The Truth about MEDIUM

Other books by Gary E. Schwartz

The Living Energy Universe (1999, with Linda G. Russek)

Other books by Gary E. Schwartz with William L. Simon

The Afterlife Experiments (2002, with William L. Simon)
The G.O.D. Experiments (2006, with William L. Simon)

Other books by or coauthored by William L. Simon

Profit from Experience (1996)
Beyond the Numbers (1997)
Lasting Change (1997)
On the Firing Line (1998)
High Velocity Leadership (1999)
Driving Digital (2001)
The Art of Deception (2002)
In Search of Business Value (2005)
The Art of Intrusion (2005)

The Truth about MEDIUM

Extraordinary
experiments
with the real
Allison DuBois
of NBC's *Medium*
and other
remarkable psychics

GARY E. SCHWARTZ, PH.D.
WITH WILLIAM L. SIMON

Editorial and production services provided by CWL Publishing Enterprises, Inc., Madison, WI, www.cwlpub.com.

Cover digital illustration/design by Britton McDaniel

Cover photography by Bob Rodriguez

Hampton Roads Publishing Company, Inc.
1125 Stoney Ridge Road
Charlottesville, VA 22902
434-296-2772
fax: 434-296-5096
e-mail: hrpc@hrpub.com
www.hrpub.com

If you are unable to order this book from your local bookseller, you may order directly from the publisher. Call 1-800-766-8009, toll-free.

Library of Congress Cataloging-In-Publication Data

Schwartz, Gary E., 1944-
The truth about Medium: extraordinary experiments with the real Allison DuBois of NBC's Medium and other remarkable psychics / Gary E. Schwartz, with William L. Simon.
p. cm.
Summary: "Recounts four years of experiments at the University of Arizona with the real Allison DuBois--the inspiration for NBC's drama "Medium"—as well as other exceptional mediums. These experiments clearly demonstrate the validity of psychic ability and mediumship"—Provided by publisher.
ISBN 1-57174-459-2 (5-1/2 x 8-1/2 tc : alk. paper)
1. Science and spiritualism. 2. DuBois, Allison. I. Simon, William L. 1930- II. Title.
BF1275.S3S35 2005
133.9'1--dc22

2005022175

Printed on acid-free paper in Canada

10 9 8 7 6 5 4 3 2 1

ISBN 1-57174-459-2

For Susy Smith
(1911-2001)

Contents

> *In order to disprove the law that all crows are black,*
> *it is enough to find one white crow.*
> *– William James, MD*

Introduction

How Science Reveals What Is Real

How we can know what in the television show Medium *is real by learning the truth about the real Allison DuBois*

It is said that truth is sometimes stranger than fiction. The question is, how do we know what is real and what is fantasy? For example, when we watch a television show supposedly based on a real life person—in this case, a purported medium who claims to solve crimes by speaking with the dead—how do we know what is genuine and what is entertainment?

The answer is we don't.

Consider an episode of NBC's hit television series *Medium* shown in the spring of 2005. The story centers around a professor at an unnamed university who conducts research on mediums and survival of consciousness after death. The story begins with the medium Allison DuBois, played by Patricia Arquette, having a recurrent dream about the disappearance of a young boy's brother near a train crossing. The assumption is made that the brother was kidnapped and killed. We are told that the perpetrator is in jail, convicted for the abduction and murder of three children. However, we are told that only two bodies were recovered. What happened to the third body?

We are shown how Allison had earlier met the professor at an outdoor picnic. With the case of the missing boy troubling her, she goes to the professor, hoping he can somehow make sense of this confusing and disturbing dream and understanding why it refuses to go away.

The plot thickens when we learn that the medium's dream actually relates to the professor, whose brother happened to disappear near a train crossing and was presumably murdered when they were children. Through a series of twists and turns we discover that the professor's brother is actually alive and has just published a novel inspired by his personal experience of his sibling's disappearance. The story concludes with Allison finally being able to sleep comfortably again, and the two brothers tearfully embracing after having been separated for most of their lives.

Is this story real? Yes and no.

NBC's *Medium* series is indeed inspired by the real life of Allison DuBois. The series accurately depicts that Allison is in her 30s, has a husband who is an aerospace engineer, has three children, lives in Phoenix, and has consulted for the District Attorney's office. The series correctly depicts that Allison is a gifted medium—she does receive information about the dead—as confirmed by four years of research conducted by a professor at the University of Arizona.

However, save for these general facts, the specific storyline about the professor and his missing brother story is fiction. *Medium* is primarily entertainment and makes for enjoyable television; it does not claim to be entirely factual. The professor who has done research experiments on Allison DuBois's mediumship abilities is me. It is true that I am a senior professor, and I do have a brother. And yes, I have spent some of my research time conducting research with mediums like Allison (although the majority of my research time over the past four years has been spent directing a Center for Frontier Medicine in Biofield Science, funded by the National Institutes of Health, at the University of Arizona.)

However, for the record, I did not meet Allison at a picnic, she did not seek me out to help her with her disturbing dreams, and my brother was not abducted in childhood. And Allison does not achieve most of her psychic information via dreams.

The problem is lack of credible information about the science related to the show. The public does not have access to the scientific truth about Allison and mediums like her. The fact is that there are a number of pioneering mediums—who for reasons we don't yet understand are more often women—who have given science some of their precious time and energy to document that what they do is real.

Real life research with mediums is sometimes so extraordinary that it doesn't have to be fictionalized to be experienced as incredible. The facts are remarkable enough. The evidence is often dramatic and sometimes overwhelming. As a scientist, I find myself metaphorically pulling out my hair as I scream silently to myself "I can't believe what I have just seen."

Who needs fiction when the truth is stranger than fantasy?

The Truth about Medium is a book about genuine mediums, not psychic entertainers or mental magicians. It focuses on the real Allison DuBois, whose life as a medium inspired NBC's hit television series "Medium."

In these pages she's joined by other mediums, including Laurie Campbell of California, Janet Mayer of Missouri, and Mary Occhino of New York. Together they have taken part in an extraordinary collection of experiments, both formal and informal, in which they have played a key role leading to exceptional discoveries.

When William James, the distinguished Harvard professor of psychology who studied mediums in the early 20th century, devised his "white crow" metaphor quoted above, he could not have had any idea he would be providing such an apt phrase to capture the success of today's modern mediums.

The truth about Allison and what she does takes on substantially more significance when combined with findings from Laurie, Janet, Mary, and others—they are white crows too. The truth about them and what they do becomes even more compelling when the striking diversity of experimental designs and contexts, conducted in the laboratory and also in real life settings, are considered as a whole. When the diversity of research sitters and their deceased loved ones are considered as a whole as well—from anonymous undergraduate students and their deceased, to highly visible persons such as Deepak Chopra, MD and the late Princess Diana—the relevance of the findings to all of us becomes self-evident.

Though this is a decidedly serious book about real phenomena, it's meant to be enjoyed, and I want you, the reader, to have fun. I have written this book in a straightforward and sometimes playful manner that even a teenager can understand. In fact, I have kept my 15-year-old godson "Skott" (yes, he spells his name with a k) and my 17-year-old goddaughter "Kim" in mind as I wrote it. With my godchildren—and even with my university undergraduate students—I sometimes get silly, and every now and again, you will witness my silliness creeping into this book.

I have written this book partly to reveal the facts about the real Allison and her compatriots as individual people, partly to describe the truth about genuine mediumship and its sometimes seemingly unbelievable findings, partly to expose certain frauds who under the guise of the label "skeptics" insidiously deceive the public (and themselves) concerning the reality of genuine mediumship, and partly to share the surprising further adventures—with their excitement, wonder, humor, mystery, and challenge—in addressing scientifically one of the most important questions about life and the universe: "Does our consciousness survive bodily death?"

Everything you are about to read actually happened. Many of the experiments were carefully crafted and tightly controlled. They were conducted in the laboratory or professional settings, video and audio taped, scored in various ways from the simple to the sophisticated, and analyzed with statistics and graphs. Other experiments were more informal, sometimes unplanned, even spontaneous, conducted in resorts and restaurants. The formally designed experiments are understandably more convincing to scientists and skeptics; the informal experiments are more inspiring and meaningful to people with a lively curiosity about the subject and those who have suffered the loss of a beloved. Together they make the controversial conclusion of this book—the take-home message—even more obvious: some mediums are beyond any reasonable doubt the real deal, and it's time that we listened to their messages and warnings before it's too late.

If you already believe in mediums and survival of consciousness after death, this book will make your heart smile. If you are undecided about mediums and don't know what to think about an afterlife, this book will open your eyes. If you believe that all mediums are frauds and that death is "ashes to ashes, dust to dust"—but you are open to changing your beliefs when faced with compelling new evidence—this book could transform your life. On the other hand, if your mind is closed but you still choose to read this book, the compelling strength of the evidence will challenge your convictions and probably give you a headache.

This is a book filled with optimism and opportunity for each of us as individuals and for all of us as a species. However, it also speaks to impending challenges and, yes, even future potential catastrophes. It highlights our pressing need to change our beliefs and behaviors if we are going to survive, heal, and evolve.

Mediumship research invites all of us to imagine a new humanity, one that appreciates the eternity of life and the infinity of love.

However, as Mark Twain noted, "You can't depend on your eyes when your imagination is out of focus." It is my hope that the extraordinary findings revealed in this book will help "focus your imagination" so that you may, as Marcel Proust said, "see with new eyes" the gift of real mediums to all of us.

Do not bite my finger; look where I am pointing.
—Warren McCulloch, Ph.D.

1 Dearly Departed

Allison DuBois provides evidence that a just-departed friend is still here

One fateful afternoon in February 2001, I was visited by a pair of ladies who had called and asked to set up an appointment with me. My administrative assistant had put them on my calendar, and I did not know who these people were or why they wanted to see me until just before they arrived. (I never did ask what they had said that won them a place on my calendar.) So I went into the meeting unprepared, at the same time feeling a chilling coldness in my heart because I was secretly grieving the recent unexpected passing of someone I deeply respected and dearly loved.

The ladies turned out to be medium-in-training, Allison DuBois, and her then medium-mentor Catherine Yunt. Allison claimed that one of her "spirit guides"—souls "on the other side" who mediums say provide them with wisdom and guidance—told her that she was "to be a part of Dr. Schwartz's research on the survival of human energy after death." No offense intended, but this was a new line for me, and I frankly would have never expected it from someone who looked and acted like her. Allison was young, vibrant, slender, and attractive, with a great smile. She was well dressed and appeared mainstream and intelligent. And tough.

She said, "My guides never steer me wrong, but I know nothing about being a research medium." Allison explained that she liked the idea of "science being fused with the other side" but she did not know if she could do what famed medium John Edward had done when he came to take part in my experiments on mediumship. She wondered if she could "pass the test." That was my question, too.

Allison and Catherine had to wait almost a month to see me. They drove in from Phoenix, and according to Allison, they were a bit apprehensive. Allison said in 2004, "If you're a psychic looking for confirmation from Gary that you're significant, forget it. Gary looks at you to study you, not to praise you. I like that about him. He's a scientist, not a groupie. I now sarcastically refer to myself as Gary's lab rat." (Since the success of *Medium* in 2005, Allison has little time to be anyone's lab rat, and she does not currently participate in our ongoing research.)

I remember the precise date and time of my meeting with Allison and Catherine because two days earlier, an extraordinary lady named Susy Smith—the author of 30 books in the field of parapsychology, mediumship, and survival of consciousness after death—had unexpectedly collapsed and died of a massive heart attack. She was 89 years old.

Allison, Catherine, and I were meeting in a room in a small converted house belonging to the university, which at that time served as the home for the Human Energy Systems Laboratory. This particular room, used for recording high frequency X-rays and gamma rays in our energy medicine research, was crowded with computers and detectors. Sitting there, apprehensive but cool, Allison DuBois looked like a well-groomed undergraduate student; Catherine looked as if she could have been Allison's mother.

Catherine explained that she was a math teacher who also was intuitive, and had been developing her psychic gifts. She claimed to have multiple abilities, including mediumship (by which she meant talking to the dead), medical intuition (making medical diagnoses psychically), and pre-cognition (predicting the future). She said she had been working as a mentor to Allison for nearly a year.

What a strange combination—from mathematics and education to mediumship and astrology.

Allison explained that she had graduated from Arizona State University as a political science major and was planning on going to law school. She told me things about herself that are now well known to millions of viewers of the *Medium* television show: she was turning 30 (though she looked to me more like early 20s), she is the mother of three young girls, and her husband is an aerospace engineer. Allison felt that her psychic abilities were evolving rapidly, but she did not know if she was as talented as the gifted mediums who had been tested in my laboratory—especially John Edward, George Anderson, and Laurie Campbell.

She was, she said, beginning to wonder if she could better serve the process of prosecuting criminals and putting them behind bars—and even making sure that murderers received the death penalty—if she offered to use her psychic gifts to support the work of the police and prosecutors. I wondered what kind of a medium would want to use her skills to help execute criminals. I was beginning to sense that if Allison was anything, she was atypical. She went on to tell me that she had the same kinds of skills as Catherine but believed hers to be more precise. And then she offered a stunner: like the little boy in the movie *The Sixth Sense*, she claimed that she could actually *see* dead people. No ifs, ands, or buts here. Allison evidenced a kind of brashness that is not common in people at her stage in life. But I should know; I had a similar quality when I was her age.

Catherine and Allison were both interested in participating in mediumship research. An idea spontaneously popped into my head: if either of these women could really do what they said, perhaps they could demonstrate it to me by bringing through information about my just-departed dear friend, Susy Smith.

I decided to do something I had never done before. I would ask two people I hardly knew, who claimed to be mediums, to see whether they could get information from a deceased person I loved. They had to make do with a minimum of explanation, along the lines of "A person who was close to me recently died." I gave them no information about who the deceased was. The person could have been male or female, young or old, local or distant, personal or professional, having died by accident or by disease. They were "blind" to any of this.

I asked them if they had any knowledge of a person close to me who had recently died; both said no. I asked if they had read the Tucson newspaper that morning. Again, no—they had just arrived from Phoenix and if they read a newspaper, it would have been one from Phoenix.

I explained that this was not a formal experiment, and that I would understand if they did not want to try. After all, they had no warning that I would informally test them that very day. They sensed that although this request was more personal than scientific, I was giving them an opportunity to provide me with preliminary evidence that they actually could do what they claimed.

They assured me they understood there would be no verbal or visual feedback until the impromptu reading was completed. During the session, I sat as completely immobile as I could; I had played enough poker in high school and college, and performed enough psychotherapy as a clinical psychologist, to know that I can keep a straight face when I need to.

Below is a summary of the primary information they each provided. As a standard for showing how their information applied to Susy, I scored it by comparing whether each statement was true for Susy, and whether it was true for my two beloved deceased grandmothers, Esther and Gussie. My grandmothers, in other words, became a kind of stand-in for "everybody else of a grandmother-age."

The truth is that if I hadn't been there and experienced this myself, I would have been highly skeptical. And even having been there, and knowing that it took place, I still find it hard to believe.

Allison

The reading began with Allison. She said:

1. There was a deceased grandmother.

Yes, there was (Susy had called herself my "adopted" grandmother), but this does not distinguish among Susy, Esther, and Gussie. Score (checkmark indicates the statement was true for that person):

	Esther	Gussie	Susy
	✔	✔	✔
Running Totals	1	1	1

2. The woman was short.

Again correct, but Esther was short as well.

	Esther	Gussie	Susy
	✔		✔
Running Totals	2	1	2

3. The woman was surrounded by flowers, especially roses.

True for Susy (she painted flowers, including roses) and Gussie (who also painted flowers), false for Esther.

	Esther	Gussie	Susy
		✔	✔
Running Totals	2	2	3

4. She died quickly of some cause associated with the chest area.

This is more specific and unique. Susy did die quickly from a heart attack. Esther was depressed and may have committed suicide; Gussie died in her 90s, peacefully, in a nursing home. Although eventually all three women's heart's stopped, the information fits Susy precisely. True for Susy, false for Esther and Gussie.

	Esther	Gussie	Susy
			✔
Running Totals	2	2	4

5. She cared about the sitter, but used to tease him.

The "sitter" being the person for whom the reading was being done—me. Yes, Susy would tease me, sometimes pointedly. Esther and Gussie were playful, but I do not remember them ever teasing me. True for Susy, false for Esther and Gussie.

	Esther	Gussie	Susy
			✔
Running Totals	2	2	5

6. The grandmother was in the presence of a young deceased child.

Neither Esther nor Gussie had a young deceased relative or other child they were close to at the time of death who might have become a companion "on the other side." However, Susy had told me that when she passed, her plan was to take care of an infant or young child who died. True for Susy, false for Esther and Gussie.

	Esther	Gussie	Susy
			✔
Running Totals	2	2	6

7. "She is showing me a newspaper. That's very strange."

Very strange indeed. In the hundreds of research readings I have witnessed, I cannot remember another one including such a comment. Not only had Susy been a newspaper reporter, but the obituary she had written herself in preparation for her ultimate passing had been published in the Tucson newspaper that very day (though I was not aware of this fact at the time of the reading). Esther and Gussie both read newspapers. However, this item clearly fits Susy. Given its obvious salience to Susy, true for Susy, false for Esther and Gussie.

	Esther	Gussie	Susy
			✔
Running Totals	2	2	7

Seven statements that accurately applied to Susy, only two that accurately applied to Esther, and the same for Gussie. The number of true items out of seven is 100 percent for Susy versus 29 percent for Esther and Gussie.

Catherine

In Catherine's reading, she confirmed what Allison had said. But since Catherine was present when Allison reported the information, it would have been inappropriate to score the information a second time. Catherine did, though, offer some unique information.

1. In the newspaper was an obituary that was significant to you.

Though I didn't know it at the time, this turned out to be a "wow" statement. Not only had Susy written the obituary herself five years before, but I had personally forwarded it to the executor of her estate on Monday to have published in the newspaper. At the time the reading occurred, I had not yet purchased Tuesday's *Arizona Daily Star* to see if it had been published. (It was.) True for Susy, false for Esther and Gussie.

	Esther	Gussie	Susy
			✔
Running Totals	0	0	1

2. The deceased grandmother had an unpublished manuscript, completely written, that you are aware of.

Susy did have an unpublished book manuscript—a novel about the afterlife—which would have been her 31st book had she lived. She had written this novel for me as a present for my 54th birthday. Only a colleague, a few of Susy's friends, and I knew of this manuscript.

	Esther	Gussie	Susy
			✔
Running Totals	0	0	2

3. The deceased wanted this manuscript published, in her honor.

I knew that Susy's desire was to have this book published. Curiously, I had that very morning thought about possible ways to have her novel published posthumously (though in the end I never followed through with this plan). True for Susy, false for Esther and Gussie.

	Esther	Gussie	Susy
			✔
Running Totals	0	0	3

4. "My guides are telling me that Allison has one more piece of information to share."

Catherine's guides were telling her that Allison had one more piece of information to share? Strange, but in fact, this turned out to be true. (See below.) The words she spoke were profoundly meaningful for me, and fit Susy precisely. True for Susy, false for Esther and Gussie.

	Esther	Gussie	Susy
			✔
Running Totals	0	0	4

So four of Catherine's statements were true for Susy, and none were true for either Esther or Gussie. 100% for Susy versus 0% for Esther and Gussie.

Allison's Additional Message, as Predicted by Catherine

In her book *Don't Kiss Them Goodbye,* Allison wrote of this moment, "I was really nervous. Dr. Schwartz is Harvard educated and taught at both Harvard and Yale. He is a well-respected scholar and I wanted to exceed his expectations of me." What happened next certainly exceeded my expectations.

Allison chimed in immediately and said, "The deceased is telling me, over and over, that I must share the following: 'I don't walk alone.'"

As I wrote in my Foreword to Allison's book, when I heard those words, it took great effort to suppress my tears. Susy had been in a wheelchair for over 20 years, and she had been convinced that after she passed, she would be able to walk again—freed at last from her wheelchair and her heavy electric three-wheel scooter. It sounded just like something Susy would say. From the unexpected reading, I was experiencing joy, sadness, wonder, gratitude, hope, confusion. And fear.

Why fear?

Was I afraid that Susy would haunt me? No, quite the contrary—I was thrilled by the possibility that Susy's dream might come true—that she would now have the opportunity to "prove that I am still here." If this meant that I would have the privilege to continue to work with her from the other side, this would be a gift of gifts. I felt this way especially because I had not been brave or wise enough, while she was alive (in the physical), to ask her all the questions I could and should have asked. She was in many respects a professional mentor as well as a special adopted grandmother. If I actually had the opportunity to continue our relationship, I would be brave enough to do so—even if this meant enduring hissing from some of my cat-like colleagues.

One reason for my fear was that it might turn out I had been duped by Allison and Catherine. I wondered, could Allison and Catherine have found out about Susy's death? Could they have known I was going to ask them to do a reading? Even though I had no conscious plan to do so prior to our meeting—since I did not know ahead of time that I would be meeting with two new purported mediums—could they have guessed that I might test them and had planned accordingly? I couldn't be sure.

I also feared that I might have been duping myself. Even though the information seemed clearly to fit Susy more than Esther or Gussie, I wondered if I might somehow have been biased in scoring the information. Since I had carefully taken notes during the Allison-Catherine reading, I knew that most of what I recorded was accurate. However, I also knew about self-fulfilling prophecies and self-confirming biases. I needed to be sure that I was not deluding myself about whether Allison and Catherine were real, and whether they were really getting information from Susy.

A key requirement in science is replication. I soon arranged to informally test two additional mediums who had recently been recommended; meanwhile a third, Mary Ann Morgan, was tested by my administrative assistant, Sabrina Geoffrion. Mary Ann's session was conducted long distance over the telephone; she did not know who the deceased person was, yet obtained detailed information so striking that I included it in an article in a scientific publication.

One of my favorite pieces of information from Mary Ann was her statement that she saw the deceased woman dancing with a man, and she heard the name "William James." I was shocked. Susy had told me, in confidence, that her first wish upon passing was to be able to spend the next year of her life dancing with William James! No one, including Sabrina, knew this.

When Allison had said "I don't walk alone," I had secretly wondered, "Was Susy dancing—which is 'walking' to music—with William James?"

Did My Uncle Sid "Drop in" as Well?

During that first unplanned Allison reading of Susy, someone uninvited had made an appearance; in the research literature on survival, he would be called a "drop-in." This is how Allison remembers it, in her own words:

While Gary was talking, I saw a spirit standing next to him. "Great!" I thought. "What if he doesn't want to hear from a relative right now?" Sometimes those on the other side can be impatient.

(As a sidelight, the statement makes it clear Allison did not think the primary person she was reading—Susy—was a blood relative of mine.)

The male spirit pulled out a wrench and started tapping Gary on the head with it. It was so funny I could hardly keep a straight face. I was also trying hard to listen to Gary's words of wisdom. Finally, I couldn't concentrate any longer.

(I had no awareness of this at the time, and certainly no feeling of being hit on the head.)

Allison continued:

Gary, there is a man that is with you, either your uncle or your great-uncle. He's not an academic like you. He's holding a wrench in his hand and he's tapping you on the head in a teasing manner. He's mechanical. He works with tools and is good at fixing things. He's a down-to-earth kind of guy.

She remembers me saying:

"Yes, that's fine. We'll talk about that after I test you."

After Allison and Catherine finished the reading concerning Susy, and I gave them feedback about their surprising accuracy, I confessed to Allison that I did have an uncle who used to joke around with me when I was a child. This was Gussie's son-in-law. He owned a hardware store filled with tools and he was very mechanical. He was good at fixing things. He was also a big tease—quite clown-like at times—and he was definitely not an academic. The information Allison provided fit my playful and often silly uncle Sid like a well-tailored suit.

Did I expect my Uncle Sid to show up—or more accurately, did I expect at that moment that I would be hearing information about a relative who had died more than 20 years ago who sounded just like my Uncle Sid? Talk about surprises!

You may be wondering if Allison could have been reading my conscious mind. Answer: not a chance, at least concerning Sid. I had not thought about my late Uncle Sid for at least 10 years, and I was certainly not thinking about him then.

Could Allison have planned ahead of time to present me with novel information about my Uncle Sid that she had somehow secretly learned about on the Web or through the efforts of a detective? I asked myself these questions and realized that although this was possible in theory, the probability that it actually happened was miniscule.

In a funny way, after Allison "saw" a dead man standing next to me who sounded very much like my funny Uncle Sid, and I thought about it later, this helped reduce my fear that I was being duped by Allison or by myself. Of course, I was well aware that only controlled research would tell for sure, one way or another. The proof would be in the pudding, carefully cooked and served under laboratory conditions.

After four years of research with Allison, there is little question that she can get detailed and highly specific information about deceased loved ones under experimental conditions where all reasonable opportunities for fraud have been effectively eliminated.

Surprises, surprises, and more surprises. I was getting prepared. Seemingly incredible adventures involving Allison and Susy, and a cast of characters both "here and there," were just beginning.

If there is one overall conclusion I have come to after 10 years of challenging and controversial research on the topic of life after death, it is this: "Be prepared for surprises." I have begun to wonder whether the metaphysical question "Can we survive bodily death?" should be replaced with the more practical question "Can we survive life's surprises?"—especially surprises that stretch our minds beyond anything we have imagined. Mediumship research is figuratively swamped with surprises.

I sometimes wonder—a bit tongue-in-cheek—if mediumship research will be the death of me.

Common sense and a sense of humor are the same thing, moving at different speeds. A sense of humor is just common sense, dancing.
—William James, MD

2 More from Susy Smith

How Allison's informal reading was anticipated by medium Laurie Campbell

Allison DuBois's encounter with Susy Smith was the second such encounter I had had in just two days.

I had met Susy Smith in 1995 when she was 83 and was already restricted to a wheel chair, in severe pain, and hoping to die. Susy was a journalist by training, and had completed part of her undergraduate education at the University of Arizona. She had carefully written her own obituary detailing her extensive writing and research experience. She insisted on reading it to me out loud—which was a first for me. As I describe in *The Afterlife Experiments*, and as Susy writes much more playfully and irreverently in her 30th book *The Afterlife Codes*, she made the decision to remain "in the physical" so she could help "prove" (her word, not mine) in the laboratory—to me and the world—that survival of consciousness was real.

Susy eventually became my "adopted grandmother" and began to call me her "illegitimate grandson." She insisted that I read many of her books, and it was hard to argue with her. Though I attempted at times to disagree with her, more often than not she won. Thanks to Susy, I was brought up to speed concerning the history of research with mediums in the 20th century. Not only did Susy know the experimental evidence backwards and forwards, she personally knew many of the key players—both scientists and psychics.

Though Susy didn't like to advertise this fact, she was a well-trained medium in her own right. She claimed to be an honest-to-God psychic who was devoted to researching what genuine mediums do. She embodied a science-minded medium.

Susy knew more about fraud, magician's tricks, and fake psychics than today's professional skeptics such as the man who styles himself as the "Amazing Randi" and who foolishly and fallaciously assumes that all mediums must be cheats. Privately Susy would become incensed about super-skeptics such as James Randi, Paul Kurtz, or Michael Shermer who made such "ignorant and stupid" claims. (Susy's words, not mine; I tend to be more reserved.) Though Susy could be tactful, graceful, and even charming in public, she could also be embarrassingly biting and blunt in private. She did not suffer fools lightly. She knew through extensive firsthand experience that mediums were like lawyers. Yes, it's true that some lawyers cheat and some are reprehensible—but this does not mean that all lawyers are frauds. Many lawyers have integrity. Many are devoted to truth. The same applies to mediums.

Susy held strong opinions about people working in the mediumship field. There were those she admired, and those she despised. She was super-sensitive as well as very tough. Some unfortunates moved from Susy's grace to Susy's wrath. For others, she became a role model, and then a trustworthy afterdeath "guide" to a number of mediums who have worked in my laboratory. Laurie Campbell, Allison DuBois, Janet Mayer [www.janetmayer.net], and Debbie Martin swear that Susy plays a significant role in their professional and personal lives.

Susy was fond of saying that she couldn't wait to die "so that I can prove I'm still here."

She was someone I adored and deeply admired, and I understood why some psychics and scientists considered her "the matriarch of survival research." She is an unsung hero in this field. However, I had no idea how prescient her "proof" words would become when she unexpectedly "passed."

I have put the word "passed" in quotes quite purposely. Susy loved editing, and she was a stickler for words and phrases. As you are about to learn, though Susy may have "passed," she did not "pass away." In fact, the evidence strongly points to her continuing to surprise us to this day, giving new meaning to the phrase, "Our work is never done." She seems busier now than ever.

I will never forget that Sunday night when I innocently played and replayed the phone message on my answering machine announcing that Susy had literally "dropped dead." I was numb. I could not believe what I was hearing. She had been looking forward to celebrating in June her upcoming 90th birthday in the lab. Now there would be no party.

Up to this point in afterlife research, I had served mostly as an "observing experimenter," witnessing mediums do readings with other people. However, when Susy died, I quickly realized that I needed to become a "research sitter." I felt a personal as well as professional responsibility to determine if mediums could obtain veridical information about my "adopted grandmother" who was both an accomplished medium and a sophisticated survival-of-consciousness scholar.

Fortuitously, my then-research partner and I were in the process of conducting a novel long-distance telephone double-blind mediumship experiment. The experimenter, Dr. Linda Russek, was in Tucson; the medium, Laurie, was in Irvine, California; and the sitter could be anywhere in the country. The study design required that Laurie not only be blind to the identity of the sitter, but also not allowed to speak with the sitter. My research partner served as both the experimenter and "proxy" sitter. This design provided the perfect opportunity for me to be a secret research sitter since the sitter never spoke.

Dr. Russek scheduled a double-blind reading for the next Monday night. It turned out that Laurie was available, and had not been told that Susy had just died. She was also, of course, kept uninformed that the secret sitter for the Monday night reading would actually be me.

Below is the complete set of 23 pieces of information that Laurie provided during the reading. As you scan these items, remember that Laurie did not know that I was the secret sitter and that I wanted to hear from one particular deceased. Also, watch carefully how the information moves from being relatively general and vague to becoming more specific and unique.

You may be wondering, how specific was this information regarding my adopted grandmother, Susy, compared with my biological grandmothers, Esther and Gussie? (As already mentioned, I was blessed to have two grandmothers I dearly loved.)

What I did that transformative night was use the simplest of scoring systems—true or false—and scored each item separately for Susy, Esther, and Gussie. Though admittedly crude compared with the sophisticated scoring methods my lab and I use today, the procedure works well when used carefully.

Here are the results of the Laurie Campbell reading.

1. There was a grandmother figure.

Obviously this is not an especially unique statement; most people in their mid-50s have deceased grandmothers. On the other hand, Laurie could have said there was a deceased grandfather or parent. (Both my parents are deceased as well as my grandparents.) Remember that the experimenter provided no feedback to Laurie about whether she was correct or not. Score (as before, a checkmark indicates "True" for this statement):

	Esther	Gussie	Susy
	✔	✔	✔
Running Totals	1	1	1

2. She had white hair, short.

Again, this is not terribly unique—many grandmothers have gray hair. However, the statement was true for Susy; false for Esther, whose hair was long; and true for Gussie.

	Esther	Gussie	Susy
		✔	✔
Running Totals	1	2	2

3. She was short.

True for Susy and Esther, false for Gussie, who was tall for her generation.

	Esther	Gussie	Susy
	✔		✔
Running Totals	2	2	3

4. She wore long dresses.

This is common attire for grandmothers, especially for their generation.

	Esther	Gussie	Susy
	✔	✔	✔
Running Totals	3	3	4

5. When she was younger, she had auburn/red hair.

This is clearly more specific and unique. The description fit Susy, but both of my grandmothers had brown hair.

	Esther	Gussie	Susy
			✔
Running Totals	3	3	5

6. She had trouble with her legs and feet; the medium envisioned her "shuffling" when she walked.

This is often common for elderly people, but it was very descriptive of Susy, wheelchair bound and suffering extreme difficulty in walking, able to shuffle only a few steps at a time. Esther walked well until the time of her death. Gussie began having trouble toward the end of her life, so the statement was true for her as well.

	Esther	Gussie	Susy
		✔	✔
Running Totals	3	4	6

7. She died recently, within the past six months.

Score: True for Susy, false for Esther and Gussie (who had died many years ago).

	Esther	Gussie	Susy
			✔
Running Totals	3	4	7

8. She cared deeply about meditation.

This statement, repeated several times by various mediums concerning Susy, was again specific and unique. Alone among the three deceased women, Susy wrote about meditation often in her books, and she learned to meditate herself as part of her training as a medium. True for Susy, false for Esther and Gussie.

	Esther	Gussie	Susy
			✔
Running Totals	3	4	8

9. She got involved with vitamins and herbs toward the latter part of her life.

True for Susy, false for Esther and Gussie.

	Esther	Gussie	Susy
			✔
Running Totals	3	4	9

10. She loved food, particularly simple foods.

True for Susy, Esther and Gussie. They all loved food, especially simple foods. Though I never tasted Susy's cooking, Esther and Gussie were great cooks.

	Esther	Gussie	Susy
	✔	✔	✔
Running Totals	4	5	10

11. She had a passion for flowers.

I was struck that both Laurie Campbell and Allison DuBois reported the love of flowers. For Laurie, the sensation was so strong that she reported actually *smelling* flowers. But this piece of information wasn't accurate only for Susy; it was accurate as well for Gussie, even if in an indirect sense. Neither Susy nor Gussie was a gardener, but both spent time painting, and both used flowers as a subject. Score: True for Susy, false for Esther, and true for Gussie.

	Esther	Gussie	Susy
		✔	✔
Running Totals	4	6	11

12. The medium saw the subject dancing.

Another striking correspondence, with Laurie and Mary Ann both mentioning dancing, and Allison stating "I don't walk alone." Even more striking, Laurie reported that the sitter would know the mention of dancing was important. As pointed out in the previous chapter, one of Susy's secret three wishes, told to me in confidence, was that she wanted to spend the first year after she died "dancing with William James." Susy had claimed to be in regular conversation with the famous deceased Harvard professor for almost 40 years, and she had written two books, both published, which she believed had been dictated to her by him, with Susy providing editing and commentary.

Before being confined to the wheelchair, Susy had loved to dance; she had been missing the pleasure for years, and was expecting to take it up again after death. And with William James, no less.

	Esther	Gussie	Susy
			✔
Running Totals	4	6	12

If we convert to percentages the total number of true items thus far, Susy has 100, Esther has 33, and Gussie 42. Hmmm …

13. Laurie saw the person with a newborn baby, and said that the sitter would know why this was important.

The second of Susy's three wishes was to raise an infant or child who had died; she never had children or grandchildren of her own. She confessed to me, again confidentially, that this was one of her secret dreams after she died. Esther and Gussie both had multiple children and grandchildren, and would have had no reason to "adopt" a newborn in the afterlife. True for Susy, false for Esther and Gussie.

	Esther	Gussie	Susy
			✔
Running Totals	4	6	13

14. Laurie saw the person surrounded by people who were "watchers" and gave many names, including Robert, William, and Edward.

Susy wrote about many people with such names in her books; she claimed that many people she knew in this life were waiting for her to die so that together they could help communicate from the other side a secret phrase that she had set up for this purpose. However, both Esther and Gussie also knew people, including family members, who died with such names. True for all three.

	Esther	Gussie	Susy
	✔	✔	✔
Running Totals	5	7	14

15. Laurie heard an unusual name that sounded like "Osborne."

This is a very rare response for a medium to make in a reading. It is highly specific and unique. Susy's second book, *The Mediumship of Mrs. Leonard*, was a biography of one of England's most celebrated and investigated mediums; her middle name is Osborne. Still, if the name had been a common one, I would not have paid attention. But Osborne is too unusual to overlook.

	Esther	Gussie	Susy
			✔
Running Totals	5	7	15

16. Laurie saw the grandmother as spending time in California, New York, and England, and traveling extensively.

Susy did spend time in all those places, plus many others. Esther and Gussie rarely traveled.

	Esther	Gussie	Susy
			✔
Running Totals	5	7	16

17. Laurie reported the specific names Elizabeth and Margaret one after the other.

Although these are common names, Elizabeth is the name of Susy's mother, with whom she was purportedly in contact for 45 years after her mother's passing. Elizabeth and Susy shared a dear friend named Margaret. There was no one named Elizabeth or Margaret associated with my family.

	Esther	Gussie	Susy
			✔
Running Totals	5	7	17

18. Laurie said that this woman was an inspiration; she mentioned this repeatedly.

Susy was a pioneer, devoted to research in parapsychology and the survival hypothesis. Even at her last book signing, at Borders in February 2001, at age 89, she inspired her audience. Esther and Gussie were very special grandmothers; however, the term "an inspiration" does not accurately portray them.

	Esther	Gussie	Susy
			✔
Running Totals	5	7	18

19. Laurie mentioned substantial information about this woman being interested in quantum physics, science, eternity timelessness, and the like.

Susy became interested in the topic of survival after reading Stewart Edward White's classic *The Unobstructed Universe*, which deals substantially with these topics. Susy emphasized physics in the first chapter of *The Afterlife Codes*.

	Esther	Gussie	Susy
			✔
Running Totals	5	7	19

20. Laurie mentioned seeing William James at various times in the reading.

As mentioned above, Susy claimed to be connected with the late William James. My grandmothers, who had not gone to college, likely had never heard the name.

	Esther	Gussie	Susy
			✔
Running Totals	5	7	20

21. Laurie was surprised that my partner's father, Dr. Henry I. Russek, asserted himself in the conversation a couple of times, and she commented on this. ("I don't understand why your father is showing up in this reading.")

As reported in *The Afterlife Experiments*, Susy supposedly received communication from my research partner's father. There was no known association between my grandmothers and the late Dr. Russek.

	Esther	Gussie	Susy
			✔
Running Totals	5	7	21

22. Laurie mentioned a few times that something to do with this sitter was a "big key" to research in this area.

This is an interesting choice of words because the cover of Susy's *The Afterlife Codes* shows a large skeleton key. Also, Susy could be a "big key" to future afterlife research.

	Esther	Gussie	Susy
			✔
Running Totals	5	7	22

23. Laurie commented at one point, "I don't understand this, but this reading is less like a reading and more like a book!"

Susy's life was books. However, Esther and Gussie were both readers. Both of my grandmothers had a strong interest in education. True for Susy, Esther, and Gussie.

	Esther	Gussie	Susy
	✔	✔	✔
Running Totals	6	8	23

Again converting the final scores to percentages, Susy ended with a score of 100 while Esther and Gussie both had well below "average"—26 and 35 percent respectively.

Try putting yourself in my shoes. Imagine that a "grandmother figure" you dearly loved had died, and 24 hours after her passing you were present during an experiment where a medium reported detailed information that fit Susy like a glove. Not only that, imagine that the medium was receiving this information almost a thousand miles away, over the telephone. You know that the medium has received absolutely no feedback from you—and as far as you could tell, she did not receive feedback from the "proxy sitter" who ran the experiment.

How would you feel? What would you conclude? Would you be skeptical? Would you be certain that somehow fraud must have been involved?

Even though I had worked with Laurie Campbell for four years by then, and I had come to the conclusion based upon numerous laboratory experiments that Laurie had great integrity and passed every controlled test I had subjected her to, I still asked myself "Could this be real, or was Laurie somehow pulling the wool over my eyes?" I even entertained the extraordinarily remote possibility that my former research partner, throwing scientific principles to the wind, might have secretly called Laurie and staged the whole experience.

If fraud was not involved, could Laurie have been reading my mind, even though she did not know that I was secretly listening in on a muted telephone? Could she have been reading my research partner's mind? Could Laurie have been reading the so-called "zero-point-field," a contemporary concept in physics that suggests that information might be stored externally in the "vacuum" of space? Or was Susy actually communicating with us?

Surprises involving Susy, as you will see, were just beginning.

The Many Lives of Mediums and Cats

Susy, as a medium, lay scientist, and skilled bridge player, taught me many things. One lesson that she taught me, in spades, was that it takes a special combination of social and management skills, plus a significant dose of playfulness and humor, to collaborate effectively with extraordinary psychics as well as with the scientists who investigate and critique them.

Genuine mediums—especially highly gifted ones—are a relatively rare genre of human beings. They can be likened to William

James's "white crows." They share traits, too, with certain familiar animals. For example, mediums are metaphorically more like cats than dogs. The cat metaphor is both playful and instructive.

I learned the cat metaphor in the process of living with two precious adopted felines—Sophia and Sadie-Rose. I rescued them from the Humane Society when they were approximately three years old. Sophia and Sadie-Rose went from being emaciated and terrified to essentially taking over my house. They meow when they want love and attention, and hiss at each other—and sometimes at me—if their privacy is being invaded. When I come home at night they can't wait to jump on my chest and purr in synchrony. It is a joy and privilege—and sometimes a challenge—to love Sophia and Sadie-Rose and be part of their lives.

Some mediums are like kittens and are easy to work with; others are more like cougars and can be trouble if crossed. Like most cats, mediums tend to be highly sensitive, are often loners, and are affectionate on their own terms. They can, so to speak, jump great heights, and amazingly land on their feet even when they free-fall. They seem to have "many lives." One minute they are purring, the next they are hissing. They can be "catty" at times and have "cat fights" with each other. Sometimes they act like "scaredy-cats" and other times they are "scary cats." They can behave like lions and tigers, or they can be like Siamese and tabbies. Like domestic animals, they come in a variety of shapes, sizes, and colors. Working with them is an adventure.

For the record, scientists are often catlike toward each other, too. Some of my own colleagues hiss at me when I talk about this area of research—and I mean *hiss*.

Over the past 10 years I have had the privilege of conducting research with an exceptional collection of mediums. In approximate order of meeting and working with them, they include:

- Susy Smith
- Laurie Campbell
- John Edward
- Suzanne Northrop

- George Anderson
- Anne Gehmen
- George Dalzell
- Allison DuBois
- Catherine Yunt
- Mary Ann Morgan
- Janet Mayer
- Christopher Robinson
- Traci Bray
- Sally Owen
- Mary Occhino
- Debbie Martin
- Doreen Molloy
- Sally Morgan
- Robert Hansen
- Angelina Diana

This group of extraordinarily gifted, caring, and genuine mediums—who have been tested under experimental conditions that rule out the use of fraud and cold reading techniques commonly used by psychic entertainers and mental magicians—have never all been in the same room together. (Cold reading is a reading done without any prior knowledge of the sitter, often using observation and very general statements to induce the sitter to confirm the statements and provide information that enables the reader to make further statements.) Truthfully, I would not want to be there. In fact, some of them complain (off the record) when I put them on the same list with the others.

I appreciate their personal concerns, special sensitivities, and individual preferences. They are, after all, metaphorically like felines. It is well known that different breeds of cats don't get along very well with each other; even cats of the same breed can have a hard time enjoying each other. Every cat lover knows that some of them are easier to give love to than others.

You may be wondering why I am presenting research with Allison, Catherine, Mary Ann, Laurie, and so forth, using the metaphor of mediums as cats. The reason is that in order to tell *The Truth About* Medium, I have to combine findings collected from multiple mediums. This includes a minority who truthfully do not appreciate being in the same place, on the same list, or even in the same book with each other. Susy was no exception.

I trust that, as I share the truth about how diverse research mediums are together providing complementary and converging evidence about the genuineness of mediumship and the reality of survival of consciousness after death, these pioneering people will celebrate their combined contributions and try to minimize hissing about being included in the same book.

And yes, I try to make the same recommendations to some of my catlike scientific colleagues. As the distinguished neuroscientist Warren McCulloch put it, and Susy reminds us, "Do not bite my finger; look where I'm pointing."

> *I didn't say it was possible, I said it happened.*
>
> *—Sir William Crookes*

3 Deepak Chopra's Father Speaks

Allison and other mediums help Deepak Chopra through a dramatic reading with his father

Unlike Susy Smith, who believed in survival when she was physically alive, Deepak Chopra believes in reincarnation. In fact, Deepak seems to feel as strongly that reincarnation is true as Susy felt that it is false. However, like Susy, Deepak believes in science. Who would have guessed that Susy and Deepak would end up collaborating on a research project after Susy had died?

In the summer of 2000, Deepak invited me to give a lecture to his "Seduction of Spirit" conference, focused on research addressing the question of the survival of consciousness after death. The lecture and our dialogue were recorded and published in 2001 as an audiotape titled "Science and Soul," released by Hay House, part of Deepak's "Dialogues at the Chopra Center for Well Being" series.

Deepak is not afraid to ask big questions. He is the author of numerous books on science, business, spirituality and healing, including the best-selling *How to Know God*. Not surprisingly, some of Deepak's penetrating questions following my lecture included the implications of survival research for the existence of God, and this point was featured on the cover of the tape box: "In the discussion that follows, Schwartz's scientific approach and Chopra's Eastern wisdom traditions converge at the same point, with both agreeing that science is a way of knowing and understanding the mind of God."

Deepak's growing interest in survival research led him to write the Foreword for our *Afterlife Experiments* book, published in the spring of 2002. However, given his Eastern background, he was understandably cautious about drawing firm conclusions. As he put it in the last lines of his Foreword: "I consider this visionary book a look-around at one of those high spots, a place where love and memory are bound together, where no one is ever lost to anyone else. A vast domain of knowledge is opened up by even the shortest visit here."

It's one thing to read about survival research; it's another to personally experience a session with a research medium—just as no flood of words, no treatise from astronomy or earth science, can substitute for actually experiencing a sunset over the ocean, be it in India or California. Shortly before *The Afterlife Experiments* was published, Deepak's beloved father died in India. One day in July of 2002, I received a surprise phone call from Deepak in California asking me if I could arrange for him to have a secret reading with a research medium. His skepticism about mediums had apparently been overcome by a deep longing to reach out and attempt to contact his deceased father.

I proposed to Deepak that, given his deep interest in both science and soul, we should conduct a controlled experiment so that he could at the same time experience firsthand what it is like to be a secret research sitter. He readily agreed.

Organizing an Experiment for Deepak

For the experiment, three gifted research mediums agreed to do the reading with him, by telephone from their own locations. I arranged to be at Deepak's office at the then-new Chopra Center, recently relocated from La Jolla to the Rancho La Costa Resort in the coastal town of Carlsbad, California, near San Diego. During the first part of the reading, the mediums would speak only with me, so that they could receive no feedback from Deepak. Since his phone number was blocked, the mediums would have no idea where he and I were at the time of testing. This was the "blind" portion of the reading.

I picked three mediums who had been successfully tested in multiple experiments using long-distance procedures, including sessions in which they brought through Susy Smith. Two of the three are already familiar in this pages: Laurie Campbell, in Irvine, California (within 50 miles of the Chopra Center), and Allison DuBois in Phoenix (more than 500 miles away). The third, Mary Occhino, would be in touch from Long Island (more than 2,500 miles away). I did not tell Deepak ahead of time who the mediums would be.

The procedure called for the three mediums to attempt to obtain information about his deceased loved ones *before the telephone reading began* and to write this information down prior to my calling them. Though this may sound impossible to you, the fact is that talented research mediums can often get accurate information about a sitter's loved ones before a reading takes place, even though the identity of the sitter is kept secret. Mediums believe this is possible because their guides bring the desired deceased to them.

Some time earlier I had begun working with Janet Mayer, a medium in St. Louis, on a novel "double-deceased" paradigm where one deceased person—in this case, Susy Smith—would be asked to bring another deceased person to a medium. Using this arm's-length approach, a medium can ask to establish a connection with the intermediary, while the identity of the actual deceased subject of the reading remains unknown to them. Susy would act as what I call a "departed hypothesized co-investigator," or DHCI—meaning that we hypothesize this intermediary is taking an active role in the reading, serving, if you will, as a kind of research assistant to the live scientific investigator.

(If you're interested in reading a formal scientific description of the "double-deceased" paradigm, with findings from a long-distance Internet mediumship experiment, you'll find details in Appendix A. The evidence indicates that this paradigm can be quite effective when used with highly motivated and intelligent DHCIs, and with gifted mediums like Allison, Laurie, Mary, and Janet.)

For Deepak's experiment, the mediums were told that the research reading involved a "high-profile" person, but were, as I've said, kept completely blind to the identity of the secret sitter. Moreover, they were kept completely blind to the sitter's location, as well as to the identity of the other mediums participating in the experiment. All they knew was that their task was to attempt to contact Susy a day or so before the scheduled telephone reading and receive whatever information they could from unknown deceased individuals who Susy would be asked to make available.

Each of these mediums has participated in many experiments with me. If any area in science requires integrity because of profound importance for the future of humanity, it is research on survival of consciousness and the continuity of life. Given that the mediums were blind to who the sitter was, and the sitter—Deepak—was blind to who the mediums were, the only way I can perceive that this experiment could have been rigged was if I personally was cheating. Just for the record, I was not. The credibility and viability of science, both mainstream and frontier, hinges on the integrity of its experimenters.

The Experiment

A date was found in August 2002 that fit everyone's schedules. Mary was first, kicking off at 8 A.M. Pacific time (11 A.M. Eastern time), Laurie did the second reading at 9, and Allison did the third reading at 10. The readings were videotaped for historic purposes with two Sony digital cameras—one trained on Deepak, the other trained on me—as well as audiotaped with a high-quality Sony micro-cassette machine.

I started with each medium by reminding her of the ground rules and asking her to state once again whether she had any foreknowledge of who the sitter was; each said she did not.

I then asked the mediums to read out loud what they had received in their "pre-read" concerning any deceased people who accompanied Susy. Once this information was on record, I then asked them to spontaneously obtain whatever information they could about the sitter's deceased loved ones for approximately 20 minutes. I reminded them that the sitter could hear the reading as it was taking place, and that they would have the opportunity to actually speak with the sitter after this portion was completed. (This was in fact done; those personal conversations with Deepak are not included here for the sake of his privacy.)

Immediately after the readings were completed, I went back to my hotel room and transcribed the formal "blind" portion of the reading—the parts where only I spoke. Returning latter that day, I asked Deepak to score the items as they pertained to his relatives and friends. Each item of information about the past or present from the pre-read and sitter-silent phases—including initials, names, causes of death, historical facts, descriptions of personal appearance and personality—was scored using a seven-point scale: -3, definite miss; -2, probable miss; -1, possible miss; 0, maybe; +1, possible hit; +2, probable hit; +3, definite hit. Items pertaining to the future were not scored.

Deepak and I are somewhat similar—we both have doctorates, his in medicine, mine in psychology; we both write; we both give lectures; we are both male; we are of similar ages; we both have deceased fathers, and we were both present at the readings. Given all those similarities, I thought it would be revealing for me to score the items as they pertained to my own relatives and friends. In this way, I served as a convenient "matched" control.

The results for Deepak were amazing, compelling, and humbling.

The best way to get a feeling for the information is to hear the mediums, in their own words, provide information that pertained to Deepak's father. Below are word-for-word relevant and representative passages from each of the mediums. I have put an (S) after each portion of a sentence that gets scored as an item.

Following the readings, I will show you how they pertain to Deepak and to me.

Mary said:

"Um, and they're making me also, this gentleman's crossed

over .... The father figure (S), he may have passed from a heart attack (S), because he's making me feel his passing was very quick, sudden, and boom (S). And he's telling me he's really good looking (S). He is, and I don't feel like he was very conceited in life, but he's just being factual (S). Is that what he's trying to say—he's making me see he's got either brown or dark hair (S), blue eyes (S), and he's showing me themselves in the prime of their lives. He says he's good looking, his whole family, he says, is good looking (S). And they acknowledge the Hamptons (S). Either the family just came from the Hamptons (S), or there's some kind of photo of the family on a beach on Long Island (S), but all of a sudden he brought me to Long Island ...."

Laurie reported:

When I see what I feel like is the father, I keep seeing the person, like, sitting in a chair and I see a lot of movement but I see him kind of self-involved in something with reading and stuff like that (S). Um, I keep having the feeling that this person doesn't live exactly where they were raised, that this person went more toward the city than the country (S). Um, that, um, something that has to do with education as well. I just keep getting the feeling of education (S) or being—I don't know if they mean more educated than the family they come from but I feel like this person kind of broke away from tradition and, um, has gone his own way in life to, um, create a life that is kind of different from what the person hails from with the family, or the belief systems are different (S)."

Allison said:

"... (W)as showing me a man of stature who has passed (S), no longer living. Um, and this person being tied to the sitter (S). Um, there was a Richard connection (S), this man that has passed, um, let's see. She was displaying beautiful women around him (S), um, he was beyond, um, I mean the feeling of this man's stature was so great that was hard to fathom. He knew politicians as well as people, um, that are well known (S). Um, there was a connection to the oil and steel industry, when, um, America was being industrialized (S). Um, and he talked about a boy and girl below him [a term mediums use to mean 'of a later generation'] that he loved (S), and that they had a small (S), um, dark dog (S), looks like it's a terrier, I'm not great with dogs, but I think it was a terrier. Um, and said there was a cremation (S) controversy (S) around him ...."

How much of this information pertained to Deepak? To me? I have prepared a simple table to summarize the items from these three paragraphs. What I have done is called a +3 a "Yes" and treated all other ratings (+2 to -3) conservatively as a "No." I also include explanations next to relevant items.

Item of Information	Chopra Score	Schwartz Score
Mary		
Crossed over father figure	Yes	Yes
Passed from heart attack	Yes	No (stroke, IV feeding stopped)
Quick, sudden, boom	Yes	No (months in hospital)
Really good looking	Yes	No (homely)
Not conceited, factual	Yes	No (poor self confidence)
Brown or dark hair	Yes (black)	Yes (brown)
Blue eyes	No (brown)	No (brown)
Hamptons	Yes	No (family to Fire Island)
Photo of family on beach	Yes	No (have no beach photos)
Laurie		
Sitting, reading	Yes	No (father rarely home)

Item of Information	Chopra Score	Schwartz Score
Laurie		
Moved toward city	Yes	No (moved to small town)
Feeling of education	Yes (M.D.)	Yes (ABD, then pharmacy)
Broke away from family tradition	Yes	No (took his father's job)
Allison		
Man of stature	Yes	No (ran a small-town store)
Richard connection	Yes	No (father had few friends)
Beautiful women around him	Yes	No (lived among everyday people)
Knew politicians and people	Yes	No (lived among everyday people)
Oil and steel industry	No	No
Boy and girl below him he loved	Yes	No (two boys)
Small dog	No	No (no pets)
Dark dog	No	No (no pets)
Cremation	Yes	Yes
Controversy	No	No

For these three representative paragraphs concerning a deceased father, there was a total of 23 items. The items were 78% correct for Deepak and 17% correct for my father. The difference statistically is huge.

You may be wondering, were Deepak and I biased in our ratings? Was Deepak inflating his ratings, and I deflating mine? This is an important question, and we were sensitive to the possibility from the outset. Skeptics correctly worry that unblinded scoring can be contaminated, even by scorers who are mindful of potential bias. Fortunately, the nature of the content itself helps answer the question. Much of the information was sufficiently detailed and independently verifiable to make the "biased scoring" explanation implausible.

For example, consider the information regarding appearance. Deepak's father was indeed a handsome man who came from an attractive family; my father was not a handsome man—for example, he had a nose like Jimmy Durante—and he did not come from an attractive family. If naïve judges who were blind to our scoring were shown pictures of our two fathers and two sets of families, and were asked to rate them on physical attractiveness, the ratings would match ours.

Commentary, Questions, Challenges

Deepak was read by three research mediums of different generations—a young mother with young children (Allison), a middle-aged mother with teenage children (Laurie), and an older mother with grandchildren (Mary). When Deepak had the opportunity to speak with Laurie and Mary, they each recognized his voice and felt honored to have read for him in this blind experiment. Allison, the youngest of the three, did not recognize Deepak's voice and had not read his books. She frankly did not realize at the time the uniqueness of this particular reading. Nonetheless, her accuracy was similarly stellar.

If you are like me, you may have some lingering doubts. Can we be sure that Doctors Chopra and Schwartz were scoring this information fairly? As a well-trained "orthodox agnostic," I apply these critical questions not only to others, but especially to myself. Some commentary and clarification are in order.

First, I was careful to make sure that both Deepak and I were mindful about rating general or common information with +3's as appropriate. This especially applied to names. For example, all three mediums mentioned that the name John was important to the sitter, and one mentioned the name Jackie in the context of John.

It turns out that Deepak was a close friend of Jackie Kennedy. That's an important fit.

John, however, is a very common name. And I have conducted multiple-experiments with medium John Edward. Both Deepak and

I gave the name John a +3 rating since it fits our respective lives. However, I do not happen to know personally anyone named Jackie, so I gave this name a -3.

Another example: two mediums mentioned that the name David was important to the sitter, and the third specifically mentioned the name Simon. A long-standing collaborator, co-author, and friend of Deepak is David Simon, MD. Hence, Deepak rated both David and Simon as +3's. The combination of these two names is obviously significant here.

Whereas David is a common name, Simon is not. However, I know a number of Davids, and my writing partner happens to be named William Simon. (This one is pure coincidence, but Bill's identical twin brother is also David Simon.) Hence, David and Simon fit me too, so I gave these names +3's. This rating procedure ensured that both Deepak and I use the same criteria for scoring a name, be it common like David or uncommon like Simon.

Because I am trained as a health-care provider, and I write and speak as does Deepak, my professional activities significantly overlap with Deepak's. This actually creates a problem. At one point Laurie said, "And being on a stage, which is weird. It's like the chalkboard thing, or somebody writing, or teaching people, or helping people. It's so weird, because I keep getting, like, life's a stage like—like we're all on a stage but we're all just doing different things, different people crossing a stage with a podium on it."

In the hundreds of readings that I have witnessed research mediums conduct, they have never talked about "being on a stage ... like the chalkboard thing." Because Deepak and I both teach—and we are both enthusiastic lecturers—we each gave +3 ratings to this pattern of information.

I should explain one other item: When I scored the readings that, without my knowing it, were actually Deepak's, areas in which there's a similarity in our professional lives naturally scored high. Laurie provided more information about Deepak's professional life, obtaining items that also described me; for that reason, when I scored how well her statements applied to me, the rating was deceptively high—45 percent. The ratings for Mary and Allison were much more in line with what we usually see when anyone scores a reading that was done for another person.

It makes sense that items not related to our overlapping professions would be the ones that best distinguished Deepak from me. For example, Laurie obtained information about a Victorian-type house, two stories, with many rooms. Deepak was raised in a large house in India that looked like this; I was not—my parent's house was a Long Island tract ranch-like house with a finished attic.

Or, Allison described a mother who "liked to make and serve tea" and made reference to there being some sort of "an England connection to her." Deepak's mother liked to make and serve tea, and she had a strong England connection; my mother made tea only when I had a cold, and she had no English connection whatsoever.

Some of the information that appeared in this experiment was spectacular for its novelty and specificity. I sometimes call these items "dazzle shots." Using a basketball metaphor, here's a dramatic "three pointer." Mary spoke of "a male who's passed from throat cancer. A man who's actually holding his throat, is making me feel he has not—has had no more vocal chords, or they removed his vocal chords before his passing." In the hundreds of readings I have witnessed, throat cancer has been mentioned maybe a half a dozen times. However, prior to this experiment, I had never heard a medium make a statement about someone's vocal chords being removed before their passing, and that the deceased was showing this.

It is not widely known that Deepak had an uncle in India to whom he was very close who had throat cancer and had his vocal chords removed before he died.

Clearly the mediums were not always correct. However, sometimes they were very close, which suggests that the error was not the information received, but the way it was interpreted by the medium. For example, Mary said, "I'm getting a father figure acknowledging a woman who survived cancer. There's someone who's still here who has survived either lung or breast cancer, because they're making me see her chest."

It turns out that Mary was incorrect in her interpretation of lung or breast cancer. I say "interpretation" because Mary did not say she was "seeing" lung or breast cancer. What she was actually seeing was "her chest." However, Mary was correct in her observation that a woman still living had survived something in her chest. Deepak's mother had survived life-threatening asthma.

At the time the experiment was conducted, Deepak's mother was gravely ill, in a wheelchair with severe arthritis and had other medical problems. Mary reported that the mother was still alive, was in a wheelchair, and suffered multiple problems.

If we rule out fraud and cold reading as being involved in this research, and we also rule out rater bias as a plausible explanation for these findings, what can we conclude?

Did Susy really bring Deepak's father and other relatives to Allison, Laurie, and Mary before the reading? Did Deepak's father really speak to his beloved son?

Or, could the mediums have somehow been reading my mind, Deepak's mind, or maybe even some holographic memory process—which from Deepak's Eastern tradition would be called the Akashic Record? (The Akashic Record is a "cosmic memory," a spiritual realm that purportedly holds a record of all actions, thoughts, and feelings from the past, the present, and the future.)

The truth is that experiments like this one tell us only whether the particular mediums are genuine. They do not tell us, scientifically, how or from where the mediums are getting this information.

Deepak had heard with his own ears that some mediums could do the seemingly impossible. He was now convinced that at least these particular mediums could get detailed information about his father and other relatives through "psychic" means. However, he still wondered whether they could really be talking with his beloved father.

The answer to this "question of questions" would come later, in the most unexpected ways.

The future is bound to surprise us, but we need not be dumbfounded.
—Kenneth Boulding, Ph.D.

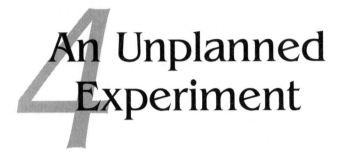

4 An Unplanned Experiment

Allison DuBois, it turns out, is also charmingly effective in unplanned, of-the-moment mediumship readings—even in a restaurant

When I was a young assistant professor at Harvard, I read a book by the late Kenneth Boulding, Ph.D., a distinguished economist and systems scientist. Boulding was both a theorist and an experimentalist. At one point he was president of the American Association for the Advancement of Science, which publishes the prestigious journal *Science*. (My mother would probably want me to tell you that this journal has published six papers of mine.)

Boulding was a big-picture thinker in science. One of his philosophical sentences made a permanent home in my mind. It is the one quoted above: "The future is bound to surprise us, but we need not be dumbfounded."

It is difficult to live up to Boulding's prudent advice when you do research with gifted mediums. Yes, I know that in science—and in life—we should "expect the unexpected." But sometimes, the unexpected is extraordinarily, even embarrassingly, unexpected. Although I try to keep my mouth closed when I work with people like Allison or Laurie, sometimes I can't help myself, and my jaw drops to the floor.

Setting the Stage—Laurie's Informal Experiment

In spring of 2001, I was in Palm Beach, staying in a charming hotel. But I was not a happy camper. Although I had come to visit a dear friend, Dr. Linda Van Dyke, unplanned circumstances required that I speak with her mostly by telephone. She was about to leave for a visit to China, and I had come down with a bad case of the flu. She could not risk getting sick. I experienced the full suite of symptoms—chills, coughing, and sneezing—with as much grace as I could muster until after about four days I began to feel better.

Dr. Van Dyke would call me a couple of times a day on my cell phone. One day my phone rang but it was Laurie, calling from California, full of excitement, eager to tell me about what was happening with her daughter Amanda, who was in her early teens at the time. According to Laurie, Amanda had started "seeing" Susy and was communicating with her.

Laurie had previously told me that Amanda was a budding medium, but she had never spontaneously reported encountering Susy before. Apparently, Susy had begun showing up at the foot of Amanda's bed at night, and Amanda was frightened. Frankly, if Susy showed up at the foot of my bed, I would be frightened too. Laurie suggested that Amanda explain to Susy that this scared her, and that Susy should appear in a safer place. Apparently, Amanda felt more comfortable seeing Susy in the mirror in the bathroom. Also, this way she and her mother could look at her together and compare notes.

I was not sure if the fever was playing tricks with my mind. At this point I should confess that I have (and sometimes suffer from) a long-standing "disease"—which some might label an addiction: it is called "science." Can science be a disease? What I mean is that whenever people tell me that they experience something or believe something, my mind takes their statement, converts it into a question, transforms the question into a hypothesis, and then starts designing an experiment to test their hypothesis. It happens quite automatically and effortlessly.

I have been practicing science since I was a child. It's sort of like playing the violin or tennis. (I did both.) The more you practice, the better you play, and the more automatic the process becomes. At some point the activity becomes second nature. It happens slmost effortlessly.

It's also somewhat like "practicing" smoking cigarettes or pipe smoking. (I did both.) The more you practice, the better you become, and you can develop a strong addictive habit. Though I am not proud of this fact, the truth is that I was a master smoker. At Harvard I even lectured using my pipe like a conductor uses a baton (and I took conducting lessons). I collected pipes and developed a deep affection for a few of them. If I had practiced the violin or tennis as much as I practiced smoking, I might have become accomplished with them. (I confess that I seemed to have more of a talent for smoking than I did for violin or tennis.)

I eventually quit smoking by the time I was 30. But I never quit science. The fact is, metaphorically I am thoroughly addicted to research—the habit is in my blood. I can't help myself. Not even when I have the flu.

The thought popped into my foggy mind that Laurie should conduct an informal experiment with her daughter. Instead of her being the research medium, she should now become the experimenter. I suggested that Laurie consider asking Amanda if she would like to try being a research medium herself. The challenge would be to see if Amanda could make contact with Susy and receive information that even her mother didn't know. Given the amount of communication Laurie claimed that she regularly had with Susy, and given Susy's substantial experience in afterlife research before she died, it made sense to try such an experiment. Laurie thought it was a good idea and said she would discuss it with her daughter.

While this was obviously not a formal university experiment, nonetheless what transpired with Laurie, and then Allison, proved to be profoundly revealing.

The next night I received a follow-up phone call from Laurie. She could hardly contain herself. Speaking very fast in a high-pitched voice, she told me how she conducted first a sitter-silent phase, in which she asked Amanda to speak freely and just share whatever she was getting from Susy. Then Laurie conducted an "asking questions" phase, in which she gave Amanda some specific questions that Laurie knew the answers to, but Amanda did not, to see if she could get the correct information.

Apparently, according to Laurie, her informal "experiment" was a surprising success. Not only did Amanda get information that Laurie knew, but she received information that Laurie did not know—information that Laurie had to look up in a book of Susy's published in the early 1970s, titled *Confessions of a Psychic,* to confirm.

I found Laurie's report fascinating. But since I was not present when she conducted her experiment and it was not videotaped, I considered what she told me as being anecdotal. Intriguing, but not science. I had no way of verifying how well Laurie conducted this experiment. I could not confirm what had happened.

The Unplanned Informal Verification Experiment

I eventually returned to Tucson and resumed my overcommitted life. Exploring whether Amanda really had seen Susy was not an item on my priority to-do list. However, the idea that some children may have a psychic gift that could be partly genetic and partly environmental kept rising to the conscious level of my awareness. In fact, the idea would not go away. I realized that Amanda might afford us the opportunity to begin addressing this complex question.

In the summer of 2001, Allison and her husband Joe drove down from Phoenix to speak to me about participating in research in the laboratory. (This was a year before the Deepak experiment described in Chapter 3.) They came to my home, and we spoke of many things. I remember sharing with them that I had many unanswered questions about mediumship. For example, it bothered me that mediums rarely got last names, even common last names like

Smith or Jones. Especially someone like Susy, who was known professionally as Susy Smith—why might mediums get the name Susy and virtually never get Smith? I suggested to Allison that if she wanted to advance our understanding of mediumship, she might consider seeing if she could develop the ability to get last names more reliably and regularly.

Over dinner at a local Mexican restaurant Allison talked about how she and Susy were developing their relationship, and an idea spontaneously popped into my head. I wondered, if Allison is strongly connected to Susy, could Allison contact Susy and ask her to verify the information she had shared with Amanda?

I didn't have a videotape recorder with me. And I didn't take notes. But I was the one conducting the informal experiment. As I recount this experience, it is as if it happened yesterday—which means that while I don't remember everything that happened, I remember much of it quite clearly.

(It's worth noting that Allison and I remember a few details differently. For example, I did not remember medium Catherine Yunt being with us on this occasion, which Allison remembers and Catherine confirms. However, the discrepancies are minor. The key facts—the important points of this experiment—Allison and I both recall the same. And Laurie recalls my follow-up conversation with her.)

To set the stage with Allison, I explained that a mother had contacted me and claimed that Susy was communicating with her child. I told Allison I did not know if either the child or the mother was correct in their experiences and interpretations. I did not tell Allison who the child or mother was; I did not tell her where they lived or what they experienced.

I asked Allison if she would try to contact Susy right then in the restaurant, and if she would be willing to ask Susy some questions. Allison was game. Not only does Allison enjoy challenges, she has a genuine affection for Susy.

I asked Allison to see if she could get answers to these questions. Who is the child Susy has recently been talking to, and will Susy describe the child for you? Has Susy appeared to the child, and if so, how? Finally, who is the mother, and what is she like?

As usual, Allison understood that she would receive no feedback from me until after the test was completed.

To look at Allison you would never know she was now doing a reading. She did not appear to be in a trance, she did not talk louder, nor did her eyes glaze over. She looked me straight in the eye and began reported what she was seeing, hearing, and feeling.

Allison said she saw a teenage girl (correct). She said the child lived on the West Coast (correct). She saw the child as large (correct). She said that the child had been very ill with cancer (correct) and had almost died twice. (I did not know the accuracy of this last statement; I later called Laurie, who told me that Amanda had been close to death at least twice with a blood cancer.)

Allison said that Susy had appeared to the girl at the foot of her bed (correct) and that it frightened her (correct). Catherine said that the child also saw Susy in the bathroom (correct) and that this was acceptable (correct). Allison said that Susy has a strong affection for this child and would continue to play a role in her life; both Laurie and Amanda later deemed these statements to be correct—but since this particular information is more subjective and deals with the future, I rated the statements as questionable.

Allison said that the mother has "the gift" [mediumship ability] (correct). She said the mother is also large (correct), and that she has been on TV (correct). Allison claims that Susy then showed her an image of Stevie Nicks of Fleetwood Mac (correct, though I did not understand this at the time; see below). From this, somehow, Allison said, "Laurie Campbell. Is it Laurie Campbell?" (correct).

I said, "Are you asking me, or are you telling me?" Allison said, "I'm telling you."

Allison had heard of Laurie Campbell but had never met her or spoken with her. Later, when they finally spoke, Laurie told Allison about a conversation she had with Susy in which they discussed how Susy wore dresses similar in style to those that Stevie Nicks wears, and how Susy and Stevie shared other similarities.

For me, the most significant piece of information occurred toward the end of our information-verification experiment. I asked Allison, "Can you give me the name of the little girl?"

Allison said she heard an M-sounding name, that it sounded like "Mandy." I was amazed. The only person I have ever met with the name "Amanda" is Laurie's daughter. I knew it was an uncommon name. To my ear, "Mandy" sounded very close. When it was time for me to give Allison feedback, I shared with her that the name "Mandy" was very close to the girl's name, Amanda, and that I was very impressed.

Allison holds very high standards for herself, which is one of the reasons she is such a good medium. Because of these high standards, she was at this point mildly angry with herself. She said something to the effect that "I should have heard an A-sounding name. I heard Mandy, not Amanda. I should have done better." There I was, complimenting her, and she was criticizing herself. As Allison describes in her book, she is very competitive, including with herself. She was a competitive skater, and seeks perfection.

After the reading, I called Laurie. I asked about the "almost died twice" statement and then told Laurie that Allison was also very close in getting Amanda's name. I explained that Allison said, "Mandy." Laurie screamed. I mean this literally. She said something to the effect of "Oh my God! Gary, don't you know that we never call her Amanda in our house? We use her nickname, Mandy!"

Amanda is Mandy? I was stunned. Allison was correct after all.

One of the reasons why I picked Allison to participate with Laurie and Mary in the Deepak experiment was because I had witnessed Allison conduct this unplanned informal verification experiment in a noisy restaurant, and witnessed her do the seemingly impossible. Yes, getting facts about a child's location, size, illnesses, and even name is powerful. This is the most solid of evidence. Since the medium was not expecting to be tested (even I, the experimenter, had not planned ahead of time to conduct a test), and certainly not under those conditions (a noisy public restaurant), it is highly implausible that fraud could have been involved.

However, getting replicated information about claims supposedly from a deceased woman she never met (Susy), who verifies that she has been appearing to a child whom the medium does not know (Amanda), is even more powerful. Of course, it's theoretically possible that Allison may have been reading my mind, since I was not blind to much of the information. However, there were certain specific details that Allison obtained that I did not know, from Mandy to Stevie Nicks. Could Allison have read Laurie's mind, a woman she had never met, in another state? The question remains open.

Telepathy, Survival, and Baseball

The design of this informal experiment does not "prove" that survival of consciousness is true. Though it is strongly consistent with the hypothesis that Susy is alive and well "on the other side," the experiment does not rule out other "psychic" explanations. However, it provides very strong evidence that not only is Allison psychic, but Laurie's daughter Mandy is psychic, too.

When a scientist sees a medium doing extraordinary things not only in a laboratory but in the everyday setting of a local Mexican restaurant, it's hard to deny that something very real is happening—though I still pinch myself on a regular basis.

If I hadn't given Laurie the benefit of the doubt and believed in the possibility that what I heard in Palm Beach was more than the flu speaking or a mother's fantasy, I would not have been open to inviting Allison to step up to the plate and see if she could get on base. Was I surprised when she hit a home run out of the restaurant!

Allison, Laurie, and others, too, (including Mary, Mary Ann, Catherine, and Janet) are like homerun-champion baseball players—without steroids.

She says she wants to continue bringing hope—wants to help people "go home" in peace. And she wants, through science, to help get the message through that we all live on. She can see things now from a broader perspective.

—Laurie Campbell's reading of Princess Diana

5 Princess Diana Saves a Life

Did the late Princess Diana really play a dramatic role in a reading?

Mediums often claim that they receive information from famous people. However, for obvious reasons, they typically do not advertise this fact. They get into enough trouble saying that they speak with deceased grandmothers (especially if they happened to write books, as Susy did) or deceased fathers (particularly if they were the fathers of notables like Deepak Chopra). Mediums typically do not reveal publicly that they regularly communicate with famous scientists like Albert Einstein or Sir James Clerk Maxwell, the 19th-century "father of electromagnetism," or with famous political figures such as Winston Churchill or Abraham Lincoln. The truth is, when mediums tell me such things "off the record," my mind spontaneously clouds over, and I sometimes get a headache. Healthy skepticism about such claims is certainly in order.

It is with substantial skepticism—modified by the reality of what actually happened—that I share with you the following seemingly incredible set of unanticipated readings. What you are about to read may push your mind beyond its "boggle factor." Most of us reach a point beyond which our minds or our skepticism says, "This is too much."

I had this experience, to an extreme, the day that Hazel Courteney, an award-winning journalist from the United Kingdom, called me in the summer of 2003. Hazel shared a personal story the likes of which I could not have invented if I tried. Her challenging phone call rang my mind's boggle-bell resoundingly and gave me one of the most severe conceptual headaches of my professional life.

As she describes in detail in her 1999 book *Divine Intervention,* Hazel became seriously ill in the spring of 1998 and almost died. During her illness, she claimed to have had a variety of "anomalous" experiences, including some that run counter to everyday experience. She says that she affected electrical equipment, began levitating, and found she was pulsing a healing energy through her eyes. And she says she also began receiving communications from the late Princess Diana. What Hazel experienced is sometimes termed in psychiatry a "spiritual emergency."

Hazel had met Lady Di on some occasions, and she says she and Diana were on a first-name basis. After Hazel had recovered her physical and spiritual health and had written the book describing her experiences, she returned to her mainstream life. She completed two health books, went back to writing weekly health columns for the leading London daily newspaper, *The Times,* as well as sporadic articles for other major newspapers and magazines, and put her extraordinary experiences behind her. Most of the truly bizarre events, such as the supposed levitating, ceased.

However, Princess Diana apparently never left her. Hazel's editor prodded her to consider writing a follow-up book detailing what it was like to return to "normal," yet transformed by her spiritual emergency. In an attempt to make sense of the totality of her experiences, Hazel turned to science, and ultimately to me. She learned that I worked in areas related to her experiences—mind-body medicine, energy medicine, and spiritual medicine—and she wanted to interview me for her new book. She hoped that I might be able to validate whether some of her experiences were real or not. I told her I needed to examine the record as recounted in her writing and see whether any of her experiences could be put to experimental tests.

In the process of reading her book, it became clear to me that one way to determine scientifically whether one of her anomalous experiences was real—communicating with Princess Diana—would be to have Hazel serve as a secret research sitter and be read blindly by at least two experienced research mediums. Would the mediums independently pick up information about the late Princess Diana? Could the mediums each confirm the unique relationship that Princess Diana purportedly had with Hazel after Princess Diana's death and Hazel's brush with death?

I arranged for her to be read by Allison DuBois and Laurie Campbell, both by this time experienced in conducting novel research readings. In August of 2003, Hazel flew from London to Tucson to participate in the first of two afterlife experiments.

The readings were conducted single-blind, meaning the mediums did not know the identity of the sitter (Hazel) or of the primary deceased (Princess Diana). Similarly, Hazel was not told the identity of the two mediums. In addition, Hazel was not allowed to speak during the reading. Although she was permitted to be in the room, she remained silent and made a point of remaining expressionless during the reading.

Yes, I could have arranged for the mediums to do the readings long distance. And I could have made sure experimentally that there was no possibility of visual feedback. However, in light of the numerous previous experiments involving Allison and Laurie that had obtained positive findings under such stringent conditions (for example, recall the long-distance Deepak Chopra experiment in Chapter 3 that had no visual cues), it seemed more important that Hazel have the opportunity to experience firsthand—albeit silently—the process of being read by skilled research mediums.

After all, Hazel is a journalist and she wanted to be able to share with her readers what it was like to be a secret sitter in mediumship research.

The results of Allison's and Laurie's readings were simply breathtaking. The readings are presented in detail in Hazel's new book, *The Evidence for the Sixth Sense,* published in 2005 (see www.hazelcourteney.com). Below is how Hazel describes a portion of her reading with Allison. For the sake of space, I have condensed the material, showing omissions with ellipses (…).

Hazel Recounts Allison's Reading

Hazel: *After 15 minutes or so the door opened, and Gary came in accompanied by a beautiful dark-haired woman of around thirty who he introduced as Allison DuBois. We nodded, as no talking was allowed. He switched on the digital video recorder as well as a back-up digital audio recorder. Allison sat down and began immediately. I took a deep breath.*

"Your mother is here. She was small but strong, and yet she had brittle bones. Liked to wear sweaters around her shoulders. She is saying honey and biscuits. Knitting, she liked knitting."

Well, this was fascinating, and I loved my mum dearly, but it was not why I had come. Yes, my mum had suffered from terrible osteoporosis during the last few years of her life. Yes, she loved sweaters on her shoulders and she felt the cold, and all her life her panacea for every problem was tea and biscuits with plenty of honey. She also loved knitting. One abiding memory I have of her was when I crept downstairs one Christmas morning at 2 A.M. to see if Father Christmas had been here—only to spy her lovingly sewing up a cardigan that she had knitted for me in secret. She was an angel.

Tears pricked my eyes. This young stranger was so far 100 percent correct.

[Mediums are rarely 100% accurate, even in segments of a reading. However, every now and again, the collections of information certain mediums obtain are exceptionally accurate, such as Laurie's and Allison's information about Susy shortly after she passed.]

"Your mother just wants you to acknowledge that she came through to us first."

The medium continued, "Mr. Brown .... There is a psychic connection here with a Mr. Brown. I'm seeing a picture of a young woman in a fur hat. Skiing—Switzerland. Oh, now I'm seeing fine boutiques in London and Paris. I'm seeing The Ritz in Paris."

I held my breath. Gary sat up straighter. And another synchronicity. Just before flying to America a friend had told me to check the Website of one Robert Brown, a psychic that Diana had consulted. And Robert Brown and Professor Schwartz have been in touch ... interesting.

[Hazel and I potentially provided nonverbal feedback to Allison when she made these comments. Because Hazel is an observant and accurate journalist, she correctly reported such movements.]

Suddenly, Allison flushed bright pink and said in her Texan drawl: "Weeeell, I have no idea what's goin' on here, and I hope I'm not wasting this lady's time—I am seeing Princess Diana in Paris."

[In fact, Allison did not grow up in Texas—she grew up in the Phoenix area—but to a Brit her accent may have sounded like that. Curiously, sometimes Allison says things that sound a little Southern to me too].

Gary simply asked her to continue as I could not speak ....

Allison went on giving me messages from Diana for almost an hour. Toward the end Gary interrupted and asked, "Please can you tell me what the relationship was between sitter and 'Diana'?" Allison's face softened and the energy in the room became very calm. "It's like they were apart—but together." And Allison brought her palms together to try to explain what she was feeling.

"She (Hazel) was brought in after I (Diana) died. Diana is saying that she helped to save Hazel's life. She is sending gratitude for the part she (Hazel) is playing in helping people to understand where we go after death. It's like she is paying homage to Hazel."

Tears ran down my face. During the fateful Easter weekend of 1998, as I faced my own physical death, Diana had indeed told me that "it had been her time to go."

...

Finally I was allowed to speak to Allison, but only to say a heartfelt "Thank you." Gary assured us both that we could chat later, once the second reading was over. Allison left as Gary let in the second medium. No one was to speak about the sitting.

Laurie's Replication and Extension Reading

Hazel's recounting, continued: *Patiently I sat waiting for the second medium and I smiled to myself that Diana had not let me down. How could I have doubted that she would? Fifteen minutes passed whilst Gary asked the second medium to "tune in," and then he brought her in. Gary introduced her as Laurie Campbell. As we were not allowed to speak, we nodded hello.*

The second reading began.

"Mom's passed—there's a grandmother coming in here. Then I see books, literature, England, spiritual matters and research—meditation, as if this person [Hazel] has something to do with spiritual matters. Travels far and wide and opening to a new reality. Needs to meditate more, which is the key to your [Hazel's] connection to Spirit."

Talk about spot-on. For the skeptics, keep in mind that we had never met. Laurie had no idea who she was about to meet, and neither did I. However, Gary did tell the mediums that I was coming from overseas, but that could have been anywhere. Yet the first country she mentioned was England ....

[Though Hazel has a British accent, she had not spoken in the presence of either of the mediums and was also not wearing any clothing that would identify her as English.]

She continued, "I keep seeing a C and a K ... and I have no idea why but they are showing me Princess Di—something about England."

Gary and I exchanged looks but said nothing. Laurie, like Allison before her, was worried in case she was on the wrong track. Gary remained impartial and simply asked her to continue.

[Again, Hazel reported our nonverbal behavior as well as my statement for Laurie to continue.]

"Okay—now they are showing me Kensington Palace. I'm seeing clothes—they were important. Outward presentation was important. They could not give a crap about the inside but on the outside it's so important. Lots of roses, she liked roses. I hope there is some connection here, because if there's none, I'm wasting this lady's time. The carpet was pulled from under her feet by her family. Her good friends became her family. She saw many psychics, but she liked Robert Brown."

It was incredible that both independently mentioned Robert Brown. And so the messages went on for almost an hour. They were very specific and detailed.

. . .

[In the following, the text in parentheses is as in Hazel's published version—her effort to make sure the reader is able to follow who is being referred to.]

And then as before Gary interjected and asked Laurie what was her (Diana's) relationship with the sitter (me).

"Well it's like a weird thing—but she (Diana) could share with her (me)—without being judged, or that she (me) was open to lending an ear, but she keeps showing me journalist and writings."

How much more accurate could it get?

. . .

Gary was becoming impatient and pressed Laurie again to clarify what Diana's relationship was to the sitter—me.

"I feel like she gave this woman a lot of words of encouragement—she (me) was like 'dead to the world'—maybe doctors thought she was dead. Like whatever she went through was like she (me) was hit by a train—she (Diana) makes out that she (me) was like flattened out. But says she (me) is still recovering. And Diana is hoping to guide her (me) ... from the other side."

After an hour, the second reading came to a close. They had both been amazingly accurate and I defy skeptics to say that any cold reader [a phony pretending to be a psychic by picking up signals from the sitter] could have been so precise. They couldn't. ***Remember, I was not allowed to speak during the readings.*** [Emphasis as in the original.]

Afterward

If you are interested in learning more details of Allison's reading, Laurie's reading, and a second Hazel/Princess Diana afterlife experiment, conducted double-blind in concert with the British medium Sally Morgan in the summer of 2004, you'll find all this in Hazel's book, *The Evidence for the Sixth Sense*. The findings from the these two surprising experiments provide extraordinary evidence concerning the ability of Allison, Laurie, and Sally to obtain accurate information under novel research conditions, the remarkable post-death connection of Princess Diana to Hazel, and the strong probability that survival of consciousness is real.

Though beyond the scope of this book, research is continuing with the late Princess Diana as well as with Susy Smith (and others), and the findings are stronger than ever. Lady Di and Susy are coming through new research mediums, such as Debbie Martin, with messages of hope as well as warnings of catastrophes.

It's belief that gets us there.
—From the movie Dragonfly,
screenplay by David Seltzer,
Brandon Camp, and
Mike Thompson

6 Believing a Triple-Blind Experment

Even with the addition of an extra layer of scientific precaution, readings are still successful

Can we believe in science? Can we trust the evidence revealed through the scientific method? Can we change our minds as a function of what science tells us?

Changing one's beliefs is not easy, even in the face of overwhelming scientific evidence. I vividly remember the conversation I had with the esteemed master skeptic Professor Ray Hymen in the spring of 2001. He confessed, somewhat sheepishly, how he had become interested in the nature of belief and its resistance to change. Hymen said that he had come to realize, quite to his dismay, that he had "no control over his beliefs." He had discovered that, rather than controlling his beliefs, his beliefs controlled him.

As a scientist well versed in orthodox agnosticism, I live my life trying to keep my professional and personal beliefs to a minimum. For example, when people ask me, "Are you trying to prove survival of consciousness?" I say, "Absolutely not. What I'm trying to do is give survival of consciousness, if it is real, the opportunity to prove itself." The truth is that we were serious when we wrote that the VERITAS Research Program is concerned with "discovering the truth about survival of consciousness and the continuity of life." (See veritas.arizona.edu.)

It is an overriding devotion to discovering the truth that motivates us to perform this research. As a scientist, my job is not to believe or disbelieve in, for example, survival of consciousness. My responsibility is to conduct research in a perpetual state of discerning openness, examining the unfolding evidence—whatever it is—as it emerges. The selective "beliefs" that I presently hold, I have come to as a result of careful reasoning and systematic observation. You could say that what I believe in are "beliefs based on evidence"—what we term "evidence-based beliefs."

Though this particular philosophy of evidence-based believing fosters good science—because it ensures that scientists remain open to all the evidence as well as the potential explanations of the evidence, regardless of how controversial or unconventional they are—it does not make one's personal life easy or comforting. I do not have the luxury of holding beliefs in the absence of confirming evidence. I am not allowed to have "faith" about scientific matters. Yes, I am permitted by this strict philosophy to entertain "hypotheses," but I cannot "believe" in them without clear and convincing evidence. This is, so to speak, the cross one bears if one chooses to remain truly open. As Chet Raymo said of Darwin in his book *Skeptics and True Believers,* "He chose truth rather than peace of mind."

Evidence-based belief is the foundation of evidence-based medicine as fostered by the National Institutes of Health and taught to medical students trained in Western countries. However, it is more easily preached than practiced. The truth is, when challenged by controversial evidence—as exemplified by new findings in complementary and alternative medicine—the core beliefs of physicians and medical researchers often bias them to reject the evidence rather than revise their beliefs.

These complications notwithstanding, our capacity to hold beliefs is profoundly important to our living and evolving. As the take-home message of the movie *Dragonfly* reminds us so poignantly, "It's belief that gets us there."

Belief is like a scalpel—it can be used for healing or killing, depending upon who is using it. As the history of humanity reminds us again and again, belief can be employed for living or dying, nurturing or killing. Science, like belief, can also be used beneficently or malevolently.

Over the years I have come to adopt an evidence-based belief in the process of science itself. I strongly believe that science, properly practiced, can help reveal what is true. Notice I say, "*help* reveal." As Dr. Jonas Salk described in detail in his visionary book, *Anatomy of Reality: Merging of Intuition and Reason* (I'm paraphrasing for clarity), "Intuition and reason are both essential for discovery as well as for understanding; they necessarily balance and complement each other. Neither one is sufficient alone for discovering truth."

It is the integration of logical science with intuitive experience that fosters the greatest advances in human understanding. They are the ultimate conceptual-experiential team.

As Louis Pasteur put it, "Great discoveries are accidents observed by prepared minds." Being prepared for surprises—including novel intuitions as well as evidence—is paramount.

The examples of mediums' experiments that you have read so far, both formal and informal, together provide compelling evidence that is consistent with the conclusion that Allison DuBois, Laurie Campbell, and other research mediums are doing something very real. Only the most ardent disbelievers (super-skeptics) would dismiss the combination of these examples as unrevealing or unimportant.

However, scientists are trained to set very high standards before drawing firm conclusions. The design of the triple-blind experiment you are about to read reflects the evolution of my experience directing exploratory and confirmatory research with mediums. The triple-blind design reflects the combined efforts of a small but devoted group of scientists—notably Julie Beischel, with a Ph.D. in pharmacology and toxicology, and Peter Hayes, with a Ph.D. in electrical engineering and computer science. Combined with my training in clinical psychology and psychophysiology, the three of us together form a novel interdisciplinary team spanning physics, chemistry, biology, psychology, engineering, and medicine.

(If you are not interested in the details of the experiments, feel free to skip to the section "Our First Triple-Blind Experiment.")

From Double-Blind to Triple-Blind Experiments

Young doctors in the emergency room learn to follow the principle, "When you hear hoof beats, don't think zebras." Don't start by assuming that the patient has some exotic or rare ailment, but consider the most probable cause first. The same philosophy can be applied to science, especially controversial science. In the case of mediumship, when someone claims to be able to receive information from deceased people, the first "horse" hypothesis would be fraud. If fraud as an explanation can be ruled out, then we would consider cold reading. If cold reading can be ruled out, then we would consider possible sitter/rater bias—the person for whom the information is being obtained is labeling as true details that are only partly correct or are false, out of a conscious or unconscious desire to believe that the medium really is in contact with his or her dead relative, or a misguided desire not to embarrass the medium.

One way to rule out potential causes as plausible explanations is to design experiments that selectively eliminate, for all practical purposes, the possibility of their occurring in the study. The key here is "for all practical purposes."

For example, it is impossible, at least in theory, to rule out "100 percent" the possibility of fraud in an experiment. Miniature electronic bugs could be secretly planted in our offices, our phones could be tapped without our knowledge, the mediums could be lying, and even one of the experimenters could be cheating. What we do, to the best of our ability, is to make such fraud virtually impossible. We set up conditions so stringent that we have exceeded the legal criterion "beyond reasonable doubt" to the point of being "beyond virtually any doubt."

For example, we remind research mediums constantly that if we ever catch them cheating, we will expose them. We remind them that cheating will destroy their credibility as well as threaten the credibility of our laboratory and its work. We tell the research sitters and staff the same thing. This is a given in our research.

Beyond that, we also carefully design the experiments to keep the mediums blind to the identity of the sitters (blind #1). Sometimes we also keep the sitters blind to which readings are theirs (blind #2).

How do we keep the sitters blind to their readings? The procedure is simple. We do not allow them to be present for the reading. Instead, the experimenter serves as a "proxy sitter" for them. After the reading is completed, the information is transcribed for later scoring by the sitter.

Imagine that you are a research sitter in this kind of experiment. You are told that a medium will attempt to contact a specific deceased person that you wish to hear from. You understand that you will not be present at the reading. A month or two later, you are scheduled for a scoring session. You are provided with two readings—one is the reading conducted in your behalf and one is someone else's. You are not told which is which. You carefully rate each item—no, I do not have a close relative named Harry; yes, one of my grandmothers was from Vienna, and then rate each item as a whole. You are finally asked to guess, "Which do you think is your reading?" You have a 50-50 chance of guessing correctly.

This procedure is similar to medical research where the patients do not know whether they are being given the active medication or the placebo. In our work, though the specificity of information is often so great that this kind of blinding is not necessary, the only way to eliminate rater bias as potentially influencing the findings is to make sure that whatever bias is present is equally operative for both readings that the rater is scoring.

The problem is that if the experimenter knows information about the sitters and their deceased ahead of time, she might—unwittingly, or even deliberately if she were inclined to cheat—give the mediums information about whether their statements were correct or not as the reading unfolded.

And that brings us to the triple-blind study, designed to eliminate this possible problem. In this approach, the experimenter who works with the mediums is kept blind (blind #3) to the identities of the sitters and the deceased.

How do we keep the experimenter blind? We employ a third person, a research assistant, who is taught which criteria should be used in selecting the sitters for a given experiment. Potential sitters are contacted about participating in the experiment not by the experimenter but by the research assistant. Sitters fill out an initial questionnaire that only the research assistant sees. One man, for example, might indicate that he would like to hear from a specific deceased loved one named Harry. He is told that he will be matched with another potential sitter—and is of course not told who this other person is. Let's say the name of this other person's deceased loved one is James. The experimenter is simply told that there is a pair of deceased people—Harry and James—and that a given medium should attempt to make contact with each of these two deceased persons. The experimenter then contacts the mediums, knowing only the first names "Harry" and "James."

So in the triple-blind approach, the mediums are blind to the identities of the sitters and their deceased loved ones (#1), the sitters are blind to which readings are theirs (#2), and the experimenter is blind to the identities of the sitters as well as specific information about their deceased loved ones (#3).

Does this experimental design give you a headache? Though beyond the scope of this book, my colleagues and I are now conducting quadruple-blind experiments that take experimental blinding one step further. Keeping all the blinding straight can produce pain and, occasionally, even nausea.

The Challenge of Conducting Double-Blind and Triple-Blind Experiments

In the history of mediumship research, double-blind studies have sometimes not "worked." What happens is that the percent accuracy scores often decrease and it may take a large sample of sitters—perhaps 30 or more—to obtain statistically significant effects.

Skeptics often jump to the conclusion that this means that mediumship cannot be real. However, a more thoughtful and less biased examination of double- or multiple-blind designs reveals a number of factors that would decrease the probability of obtaining accurate readings under these obviously "unnatural" conditions.

For example—assuming for the moment that survival of consciousness is possible—most double-blind studies do not take into account the question of how the deceased person manages to know when and where the research reading is taking place. If you are the sitter and you are present at the reading (single blind), you are most likely actively inviting your loved one to be there, and your loved one is presumably paying attention to your activities. Even if all the medium is doing is reading your mind—at least you have brought your mind with you. However, if you are not present at the reading (double-blind), how does the medium know who to ask for, and how does your loved one find his or her way to the medium?

To minimize these problems, here's what we do.

First, the research assistant tells you when your reading is scheduled, so that you can invite your loved one to be there—even though you won't be there physically. Though you won't be allowed to have any contact with the experimenter until after the readings have been completed and you have scored your data, you can think of your loved one during the time that the reading is scheduled, even if you are in class, at work, driving your car, or whatever.

Second, the research assistant gives the experimenter the first name of your loved one—for example "Harry"—and in turn she gives the name "Harry" to the medium to contact. Hence, although there is a legion of deceased people who have the name Harry, it helps narrow down the field of possibilities significantly. Since your beloved Harry potentially knows that a reading is taking place and since the medium is asking for Harry, there is an increased chance that your Harry will show up to the reading.

Third, we invite a deceased like Susy Smith who has successfully worked with our research mediums in the past (as evidenced by positive findings in multiple experiments) to help bring your loved one to the medium. In other words, we add the "double-deceased paradigm" to the triple-blind design.

You may be wondering whether we have systematically tested to what extent any of these factors play a significant role in enabling us to succeed where others have sometimes failed. The answer is "not yet." Our research program is a "work in progress"; this kind of research is time-consuming and costly, and we can do only so much with the resources we have.

Another problem with multiple-blind designs is that deceased people are sometimes similar in various qualities. For example, let's say that Harry and James are both adult males of the same generation who died when they were in their early 50s. Harry and James will likely share many things in common. Their commonality potentially increases the degree of overlap in the information provided by mediums about them, which in turn will make it more difficult for you, the sitter, to discriminate between them under blind scoring conditions.

However, if Harry died in his early 50s and James died in his teens, this decreases the degree of overlap between them. Though the experimenter knows that one member of the pair will be older and one younger, the mediums are not told this fact. And remember: the experimenter is kept blind to who is actually older—Harry or James. This procedure increases the ability of the medium to get differentiating information and also increases your chance of identifying which of the two readings fits your beloved Harry. It becomes the research assistant's task to arrange pairs of deceased people to be read and rated who differ on as many qualities and characteristics as possible.

Our First Triple-Blind Experiment

That we were able to conduct such sophisticated mediumship research is thanks to Dr. Peter Hayes, who funded a full-time position creating the William James Post-doctoral Fellowship in Mediumship and Survival Research (the same James who made the "white crow" statement and purportedly was seen dancing with Susy since she passed), and to Dr. Julie Beischel, who serves in this position.

Julie loves experimental designs and she is devoted to doing things right. She has a passion for this research that began unexpectedly when she was completing her Ph.D. and learned that her mother had committed suicide. Originally a disbeliever, she and her younger sister—who works as a research assistant in cancer studies—arranged to have a private reading with Allison DuBois and secretly conducted their own experiment. The two of them purposely provided virtually no verbal or visual feedback to Allison, yet the reading proved to be exceptionally accurate. Julie entered the reading a skeptic and left it on the path to concluding that Allison was the real thing.

After collecting and scoring their data, Julie, though at the time a stranger to me, asked if she could come and show me her findings. No one had ever come to me before who had conducted their own mediumship research, requested that multiple family members not present at the reading score the data independently, and then tabulated the results. I was impressed.

With Julie's and Peter's assistance, we designed the triple-blind experiment to use eight undergraduate sitters and initially to use four mediums: Allison DuBois and Debbie Martin of Arizona, Traci Bray of Missouri, and Doreen Molloy of New Jersey. The research assistant who helped select the sitters and scheduled the readings was Lauren Fleischman. The experimenter and proxy sitter was Julie. Each medium read a pair of deceased people. The first part of each reading was "free form": the medium was asked to describe whatever she experienced. Anything that came to mind was to be reported. The second part of each reading involved "life questions": the medium was asked to get information related to specific questions.

Julie asked four questions from a standardized script and used the word "discarnate" to refer to the deceased person—a word already familiar to the mediums:

Question One: What does the discarnate look like? Give a physical description of her (or him) including relative height, build, and hair color, if possible.

Question Two: Describe the personality of the discarnate, including whether she (or he) was more shy or more outgoing, more serious or more playful, and more rational or more emotional, if possible.

Question Three: What were the hobbies or activities of the discarnate during her (or his) life? What did she/he like to do?

Question Four: What was the discarnate's cause of death?

The final part included a single question where Julie asked the medium, "Does the discarnate have any comments, questions, or requests for the sitter?"

After each reading was completed, the digital audio files were transcribed and prepared for item-by-item scoring, where the sitter would be blind to which reading was his/hers. The following results will give you a feeling for the differences that a skilled medium like Allison can get between two deceased people whom she knows only by first name—people purportedly brought to her by Susy. The readings are identified as 3 and 4, according to their order in the series of eight readings total. The two names Allison received were females. (To protect confidentiality, the names given below are fictitious; quotes reflect actual wording by Allison. You can see how specific much of the information is and how the details differ between the two readings.)

Reading #3—Part B: Life Questions

The medium is asked four questions about the named discarnate and asked to report the answers.

Question 1: Physical description.

- She's younger, 12, a child.

- Pigtails, a picture of her with long pigtails.
- She's got "the baby."
- Someone lost a baby in the immediate family, maybe her mother.
- Marianne couldn't stay out in the sun too long, it made her skin blotchy or there was a skin allergy or freckles or something aggravated by the sun.
- She had a great smile that she was proud of.
- Her mom knew when she was up to no good because it showed in her eyes; her eyes always gave her away.
- She's thin, not largely built.
- There was a joke about her shoe size, her sneakers, that her feet were abnormally large.

Question 2: Personality.

- She was empathetic, she felt for people and animals.
- She was very loving.
- She had somewhat of a distrust for people.
- She took it very hard when someone was disappointed in her, she didn't like disappointing her mom or family.
- She was hard on herself.
- She feels like she disappointed people with dying.
- She didn't lie well.
- She was playful.
- She took things seriously only when it would affect someone else.
- She thought a lot about how her actions affected other people.
- She was not able to stop the passing, it was out of her control.
- "It was my time."
- She was intelligent, had common sense.
- She thought a lot of adults didn't have common sense.
- With family, she was more playful, more outgoing.
- She could be shy around strangers.
- Marianne at a podium, speaking to people in an auditorium.
- She would have spoken publicly.

- Her mom speaks publicly or will because of Marianne's passing and she [Marianne] is there with her when she speaks.

Question 3: Hobbies/activities.

- She liked to make people laugh, tell jokes.
- She had a joke-telling book.
- She liked to sing, but maybe "should have kept it in the shower."
- Someone named their baby after her after she died.
- Mother's Day being important, "Happy Mother's Day" to her mom, she's with her at this time.
- Something happened around Mother's Day that was pivotal for her family.
- A Christmas tree in a church.
- People speaking about her at Christmas time.
- A service around Christmas, her friends are in the church, Marianne being there.
- Pizza, this is a good thing, she's throwing open the top and picking up a big slice.

Question 4: Cause of death.

- Marianne choking, some sort of neck trauma.
- Being hit in the head and choking on the blood, so much pressure right there.
- She's grappling with how she passed. It was not a good way to pass.
- The wrong person found her; she didn't want this person to find her or see her when she died. She doesn't want to be remembered that way.
- "I'm beautiful and I'm vibrant and I don't look like that."
- It bothered her because she had to step outside of herself to see herself and she doesn't like that.
- Someone bought a lot of angels—pins, statues, etc.
- The angels are "mine. They're from me and for me."
- Angels sent to her mom or given to her mom from many different people in many different places.

- A little hairy lap dog, it looks like Toto, that breed.
- Marianne liking to mess with this dog. He knows when she's there, he barks, she plays with him and she likes this.
- Her mom or someone very close to her has the dog.
- She likes the baby.
- A wedding right around August.
- Her death was partially accidental and partially intentional.
- She's not showing someone else's hand in it.
- She didn't really mean to go, she's sorry, she didn't want to leave her family, but it was her time.

Now compare and contrast these items with those from reading #4.

Reading #4—Part B: Life Questions

Question 1: Physical description.

- Around 5 feet 4 inches.
- Not very big, petite.
- She lost weight at the end of her life.
- Her hair wasn't straight; it had wave in it.
- Her hair was brown, but she dyed it, too.
- She had light eyes.
- Green eyes are important to her, loving green eyes.

Question 2: Personality.

- She was stronger than she looked, she was a real toughie inside.
- She cared a lot about other people.
- She'd stand up for herself too, except to her mom.
- She was more shy.
- When people were having a conversation like she wasn't in the room, they wouldn't expect her to say something and she would, and they always looked shocked.
- She worried more about other people than herself.
- She worried herself to death.
- "Julie."

- She loved April.
- She's not showing kids around her, she's standing alone.
- In the end, she had to do it herself, she had to be alone.
- People tried to save her with their love; she wasn't to be saved.
- A lot of people prayed for her.
- The pink ribbon for breast cancer.
- "Merry Christmas, Happy New Year."
- He saved all the cards she gave him and it's hard for him to look at them.
- Medication being necessary for him for depression.
- She's sorry—if it was up to her, she wouldn't go. But she's still around, just in a different form.
- She's healthy again, and happy.
- She's younger, in her late 30's, like 37.
- She's sound with herself, she's not a vain person.

Question 3: Hobbies/activities.

- "Oh, I used to do a lot of things."
- She liked to take walks or jog.
- "I liked to have a good time."
- She was in bars when she was younger and enjoyed throwing back a few.
- She really liked to shop.
- She'd try anything once.
- She liked to take bubble baths.
- She liked to be in the water or to swim.
- She's sitting on a bank fishing with a grandpa, it could be her mother's grandpa.
- He would be identifiable by his love for fishing or that he was always fishing.
- He had the kindest eyes.
- He is the good-looking older man that brought her through at the beginning.
- She has a lot of family there, more than she knew.

Question 4: Cause of death.

- Sickness throughout her system, like cancer.
- It started in her chest—breast or lung.

Analysis

After each sitter blindly rated the items, they were asked to give a global rating of each reading as a whole.

The rating scale is as follows:

6—Excellent reading, including strong aspects of communication, and with essentially no incorrect information

5—Good reading with relatively little incorrect information

4—Good reading with some incorrect information

3—Mixture of correct and incorrect information, but enough correct information to indicate that communication with the deceased occurred

2—Some correct information, but not enough to suggest beyond chance that communication occurred

1—Little correct information or communication

0—No correct information or communication

The simplest and most compelling way to analyze the data is to compare how the participating sitters, the students, scored their readings and how they scored the matched control readings. Remember that they were blind to which set of information was provided by the medium in the reading with them and which was from a reading with another person.

The results were startling in their clarity. When the eight sitters scored the reading that was not theirs, the average score was 2.1. A score of 2.1 means "some correct information, but not enough to suggest beyond chance that communication occurred."

However, when the eight sitters scored their own readings, the average score was 4.6—which falls between a "good reading with some incorrect information" and a "good reading with relatively little incorrect information."

Statistical analysis reveals that the difference between 4.6 and 2.1 is $p < .02$—meaning that the possibility of this difference occurring by chance is less than 2 out of hundred, which is a "statistically significant" finding.

Allison's average for the two readings was 5.0 for the sitters' own readings and 1.5 for the matched control readings.

Let's review what this means. Research mediums like Allison can hear just the first name of a deceased person (presumably a deceased person who is motivated to participate and is brought to her via another deceased person, in this case Susy Smith). The person who is conducting the reading—Julie, the experimenter—knows virtually nothing about the deceased people. Therefore, Julie can't give any feedback to Allison, since she has none to give. And Allison can't read Julie's mind to get the information, since Julie is serving as a "proxy sitter" for the absent sitters.

Only those absent sitters know the deceased and can potentially determine what information is accurate. The sitters later come to the lab and score the information blindly. They were not present when the readings took place. Whatever biases they have, they will apply them equally to the two readings, since they don't know ahead of time which is theirs.

Nonetheless, the sitters successfully pick, way beyond chance, which reading is their reading.

This experiment tells us many things. One of the most important is that informal observations in restaurants and long-distance single-blind experiments with famous sitters provide evidence that can be replicated in super-controlled triple-blind experiments in the laboratory. When the artificiality of the laboratory replicates real-life phenomena for a given medium, it logically follows that we should treat the real-life phenomena for that medium as genuine.

Mediums like Allison can, under appropriate laboratory conditions, generate data that cannot be explained as fraud, subtle cuing, rater bias, experimenter error, or even mind-reading of the physically alive. As Julie puts it, the evidence strongly points to the existence of the "physically challenged"—the disincarnates, sometimes called spirits—as providing much of this information.

For the record, even after having written this chapter, I still find it hard to believe that it really happened, that the experiment actually worked. But it did, and it does. For better or worse, this is how the universe works.

Based on this evidence, some people will argue that it's time we start celebrating the reality of the afterlife and actively consider the deeper implications of what it means for our health, survival, and evolution, before it may be too late.

However, there are those who will say, "Absolutely not." You will meet two of these exceptionally skeptical people in the next chapter.

> *Unthinking respect for authority is the greatest enemy of truth.*
> *—Albert Einstein*

7 A Trap Foretold

Allison foretells an "ambush" by two famous skeptics

Mediums sometimes report receiving warnings from deceased people about forthcoming accidents or disasters. Though this may appear to defy reason and logic, over the past 10 years I have witnessed numerous premonitions of danger reported by mediums that subsequently came true. I have learned to take seriously such warnings from "the other side." I no longer dismiss them out of hand; I give them the benefit of the doubt.

In Janna Excell's inspiring book, *Soul Light: Connection Between Worlds*, she recounts the following story in her Epilogue:

> *On Wednesday, February 5, 2003, I made a phone call to Dr. Gary Schwartz regarding some information I had just received. The information contained potential threats for Gary regarding his professional work and, possibly, physical danger.*
>
> *At that point in time, he was working with a medium named Janet, who was channeling Susy Smith, author of* The Afterlife Codes. *He had just received an e-mail that morning from Janet who had channeled Susy regarding this potential*

> *threat. So, my call, at that exact moment, was highly significant to him. I was totally unaware of Susy's warning when I called and did not realize I had a part in a larger scenario.*
>
> *I told Gary not to worry. I replied, "Jack will serve as a spirit guide in protecting you. He is already with Susy working on this." Gary immediately responded, "Jack working with Susy? Ah, we can test that! I'll ask Susy to bring Jack through with her tomorrow when Janet channels her."*

Janna received this information in a phone call from a friend who had heard the warnings firsthand from the potential perpetrator.

Can you imagine being in my shoes on that day, first receiving a warning via e-mail from a medium in St. Louis (Janet), supposedly relaying a message from my adopted grandmother (Susy), warning me of a potential personal and professional danger? And then having that warning independently confirmed in the early afternoon via cell phone from a grief counselor in Tucson (Janna)?

Talk about a mixed blessing—receiving caring warnings from both "there" and "here," together helping me prepare for potential danger.

Janna's book provides details of the two experiments I conducted with Janet that provided surprising and compelling evidence of the threat and its "protection from the other side." But it was Allison DuBois's unanticipated contribution in coming up with evidence regarding the "trap foretold"—the incident recounted in this chapter—that probably takes the cake. The event involves two well-known super-skeptics and their plan to "ambush" Allison, another medium, and me. Even as I recount the incident here, I have an extraordinarily hard time accepting that it really happened, even though I lived through it and survived to tell the tale.

I'm not naïve regarding the tactics of some critics who hold exceptionally biased positions on subjects that they somehow believe are not even worthy of being explored. Even though I've been attacked unfairly by some of the best and brightest skeptics, as well as by well-meaning but closed-minded scientists, I was not prepared for the lesson that forced me to acknowledge how far intelligent people will sometimes go to prevent evidence about mediums from being shared honestly and fairly.

Are you sitting down? The journey is about to get very bumpy.

The Lawrence O'Donnell Fiasco

In the summer of 2003 I received a phone call from a producer in Los Angeles inviting me to appear as a guest for a possible new television series that they hoped would replace *The Rosie O'Donnell Show*. I was in New York City at the time, finishing work on my book *The G.O.D. Experiments*. The producer said she wanted me to appear as part of the pilot for the *The Lawrence O'Donnell Show*.

To encourage me, she told me a bit of O'Donnell's background. He had been an undergraduate at Harvard and among other things had been an award-winning writer of the television show *The West Wing* as well as a political analyst for MSNBC. She wanted me to talk about my book, *The Afterlife Experiments,* which presented scientific evidence addressing the controversial question of whether consciousness survives bodily death. She also wanted me to recommend some mediums who might be willing to be interviewed on the show as well. Two of the names I mentioned were Suzane Northrop and Allison DuBois.

The producer led me to believe that O'Donnell was personally interested in the topic of life after death and would carefully examine (and maybe read) the book before conducting the interview. I was told that O'Donnell was an intellectual and that he would conduct a serious interview with me about the experiments and their implications. I was happy to participate in what I anticipated would be an honest discussion of the evidence, pro and con, and its implications. I agreed to be taped for the show, which was scheduled to take place a few weeks later.

When I got to the studio, both Suzane and Allison were already there. We exchanged greetings and hugs. Allison then took me aside and she said, "Gary, Susy is here and she has a warning for you."

I asked, "What could possibly happen here?"

Allison replied matter-of-factly, "Susy says that you and I should be prepared to be ambushed."

Ambushed? Susy said “ambushed”? In front of hundreds of people, by a Harvard-educated host-to-be who hoped his television show would be picked up by one of the networks?

It didn’t compute.

However, before the show, I was introduced to the surprise “skeptic” who had been invited to participate as well—Penn Jillette of Penn and Teller, the “bad boys of magic.” I began to wonder. The producer had not told me that a skeptic would be included as part of the interview. When Penn took me aside and whispered angrily, “How can you believe those lying c__ts?” (the word he used was not “cats”), I began to become concerned. I thought to myself, “How fortunate Penn isn’t the host of this show.”

I tend to be a gentle person, especially with people I have never met. Penn’s seething hostility was palpable, and I did not know what I would do if he became aggressive in public. I knew that Suzane and Allison were both very tough felines. (Recall the cat metaphor.) I knew that Allison was prepared for a trap, thanks to the purported warning from Susy. I wondered if this was going to be the warning from Janet and Janna all over again.

My concerns increased further when the lights came on, the music began, and O’Donnell came out to introduce our segment. He began by asking the audience of approximately two hundred people, “How many of you believe in survival of consciousness after death?” About 40 percent indicated yes.

He then asked, “How many of you are not sure whether consciousness survives death?” Another group of hands, again about 40 percent.

Then he said, “How many of you are *thoughtful* people and know that survival of consciousness is *not* true?” The remaining 20 percent proudly raised their hands.

I could not believe what I was hearing. O’Donnell was introducing our segment with his conclusion before he and I had even had our interview, a conclusion that announced to the audience that his mind was already made up, since if they were “thoughtful” people (as he was), they agreed with him that survival of consciousness is not true. He was clearly implying that people who believed otherwise were thoughtless individuals who were allowing themselves to be conned by unscrupulous, lying mediums and gullible, if not deceiving, academic scientists.

I would soon discover how thoughtless O'Donnell was himself.

The first portion of the three-portion segment involved O'Donnell conducting an unfriendly and at times nasty interview with Allison and Suzane. He accused them of taking advantage of grieving people for fame and fortune. He goaded them to do a reading for him, on the spot. Neither Allison nor Suzane was willing to take the bait.

The first portion ended for a commercial break. There was murmuring in the audience. In the second portion, Penn was invited to join the mediums. He was there as the sophisticated "skeptic" and "skilled magician." He went on the attack and accused Allison and Suzane of using fraud and cold reading. Both he and O'Donnell ignored the fact that a scientist (me) was about to be interviewed about controlled experiments that ruled out fraud and cold reading as plausible explanations for what Suzane and Allison do.

The second portion ended for another commercial break. Allison and Suzane were escorted off the set, but Penn remained. Would the interview with me include Penn? I was brought out and seated next to Penn.

O'Donnell had yet to come back from the break.

Penn is huge, well over six feet tall and heavy, towering over my five-feet-seven frame. He leaned over, seemingly innocently, and whispered in my ear, "I hate you!"

What did he say? He hates me? Why? I was shocked.

I turned to him, and gently but firmly said, "Excuse me? How can you hate me? You don't even know me."

Penn replied more loudly and angrily, "You have taken my mother's memory in vain!"

I was appalled. I said more forcefully but still gently, "Forgive me, but how can I have taken your mother's memory in vain? I don't even know your mother."

Penn said, "You listen to those lying c__ts, and you even lie in your book!"

What? I lie in my book? I had no idea what he was talking about.

At that moment I felt as if I had been a bug crawling on the floor, Penn would have squished me with his foot, with glee.

Before I had the opportunity to digest his angry accusations, O'Donnell returned and sat down on my left, sandwiching me in between two closed-minded people, one of whom had already announced that he hated me. I began to wonder, "Would the scientific evidence reported in my book be given a fair hearing on this show?" And I wondered, would there be an ambush, as Susy purportedly foresaw?

Before the cameras started rolling and the formal interview began, O'Donnell turned to me and whispered in my ear, "Were you an undergraduate at Harvard?"

I said, "No, I received my Ph.D. at Harvard." *The Afterlife Experiments* book clearly states that I received my undergraduate degree from Cornell.

O'Donnell then said, "So you are not a Harvard college graduate and I will not announce your Ph.D. on the show."

I could not believe what I was hearing. I said, "Excuse me? Do you seriously question whether I have a Harvard Ph.D.?"

O'Donnell replied, "I did not check to see if you have a Harvard Ph.D., and yes, I believe you are lying about the credentials listed on the jacket of your book."

I could not fathom what he was saying. It is one thing to question whether mediums are real; it is quite another to question whether someone's Ph.D. is real.

I do not know whether he or one of the show's researchers had called Harvard to ask if I have an undergraduate degree from there, but such a call wouldn't have made any sense—my undergraduate degree is from Cornell, my doctorate is from Harvard, and I've never claimed any different. Apparently no one had bothered to ask Harvard about my Ph.D. And because they had not asked for and received that verification, O'Donnell was going to claim that I was lying about my degrees? Incredible!

I then said, "From statements you made to Suzane and Allison, it sounds to me like you have not read my book."

O'Donnell said, "That's right. I have no need to read your book. Since you have lied about your credentials, you have probably lied about the data you presented in your book!"

Despite Professor Boulding's comment quoted earlier—"The future is bound to surprise us, but we need not be dumbfounded"—I confess I had become momentarily dumbfounded at that point. Before I had a chance to digest what he had just said, the cameras began to roll and O'Donnell was announcing that his interview with me was to begin. The music came on and O'Donnell was all smiles to the audience.

He asked me to tell the audience what my current position was at the University of Arizona. I explained that I was currently a professor of psychology, medicine, neurology, psychiatry, and surgery.

O'Donnell then asked me, "Do you have an M.D.?"

I said, "No."

He then asked, "Do you teach surgery to surgeons?"

I said, "Of course not. I am a psychologist, not a surgeon."

He then said, "You know, Dr. Schwartz, that Ph.D.s can't be professors in medical school departments, and that you are lying about your credentials."

I was now doubly dumbfounded. I knew that the findings from mediumship research were unbelievable enough. But what was happening here seemed beyond unbelievable; the events appeared completely unimaginable.

I began to explain to O'Donnell and the audience that Ph.D.s from many disciplines regularly have research professorships in both academic and clinical departments in medical schools. I pointed out that medical schools have Ph.D. professors from fields including physics, bioengineering, biophysics, biostatistics, biochemistry, physiology, clinical and health psychology, medical sociology, medical anthropology, and epidemiology. I attempted to explain that this practice occurs in medical schools throughout the U.S. and that he could easily confirm my academic appointments by contacting the University of Arizona.

O'Donnell was incensed. He would hear none of this.

Clearly this was indeed the ambush I had been warned about. I went on the offensive. I asked him, on camera, "Did you graduate from Harvard College?"

He said, "Yes."

I asked, "Do you know what Harvard's motto is?"

He said, "Yes."

I asked, "What is it?"

He said, "Veritas."

I asked, "What does Veritas mean?"

He replied, "Truth."

I then said, "If you genuinely believe in Veritas, then I want you to call the University of Arizona to determine if I am lying to you and your audience, or if you are mistaken."

I further said, "I am asking you, on camera, in front of this audience that, when you learn from senior officials at the University of Arizona that the credentials listed on the book jacket are indeed correct, you will announce on a future show—if you have a future show—that you were mistaken about my credentials and that you had falsely accused me of lying."

O'Donnell replied, "Absolutely not!"

As you can probably guess, the interview went downhill from there. O'Donnell was not interested in the evidence. And he was not interested in the details of the experiments. What he was interested in was supporting his biased convictions, his "story," that I was a fraudulent scientist working with fake mediums.

As the interview progressed, it became apparent that O'Donnell was not doing this simply for Jerry Springer "shock value"—he seemed to genuinely believe that I was a liar. And unfortunately he had no interest in checking the evidence to see if his potentially slanderous story about my credentials was actually true. I wondered if the success of this pilot would guarantee him a lucrative and reputation-making place on television, and whether he had decided that exposing a highly reputed scientist to be a fraud would be one of the ingredients that would convince the network he had the right stuff for a successful show.

Thoughts about the Veritas War

There is an old, cynical phrase, "Don't let the facts get in the way of a good story"—which may be socially acceptable when you're telling an entertaining story at a dinner party but is intellectually corrupt and appalling when you're speaking to what you hope will be a television audience of millions.

I recognize that many intelligent, reasonable people do not yet believe that survival of consciousness is true. O'Donnell was apparently not interested in examining the scientific evidence addressing life after death, much less considering the big philosophical and spiritual questions of an afterlife.

The experience proved to be an object lesson in how strong beliefs about a very emotional topic (in this instance, the possibility of an afterlife) can so cloud our judgments that we will no longer remain open to evidence of things that we can easily confirm or refute—such as whether Gary Schwartz holds professorships in the University of Arizona College of Medicine or not.

I wondered, what is it that motivates people like O'Donnell to close their minds to questions—especially trivial questions that can be easily answered?

Einstein put it this way, "The important thing is not to stop questioning." Einstein recommends that we should always remain open to new data and new ideas.

Although O'Donnell did not know it, he unwittingly gave me a gift, and I genuinely thank him for this. He showed me that in certain circumstances it is necessary for people who care about truth to become at times warriors for the truth. Simply put, what might be called "the Veritas War" had begun for me in a TV studio in Los Angeles.

O'Donnell was clearly angry with me. He became furious when I told him after the interview that I felt sorry his convictions were so strong that he would not be willing to seek information that could confirm or disconfirm his cherished beliefs.

O'Donnell had unwittingly handed me a priceless take-home lesson: just because someone is clearly intelligent and highly educated—even graduating from Harvard College—does not mean that she or he will be open to information and will practice evidence-based living.

Have you met any people like O'Donnell? Have you watched any people like O'Donnell on television? Do you, consciously or unconsciously, practice an O'Donnell-like approach to some subjects? If truth matters, it's time to stand up and say at least on some occasions that the people like O'Donnell are, like the emperor in the fable, not wearing any clothes.

I was extraordinarily grateful that Allison had received information, apparently from Susy, warning us to be prepared for an ambush. Because I had been forewarned by information attached to Susy—and I had been previously forewarned via other mediums by information also attached to Susy—I was better prepared to cope with a frankly crazy situation, one I could never have imagined.

Aftermath

Talk about surprises: in the end, poetic justice prevailed. As O'Donnell and Penn left steaming, and the majority of the audience walked away seemingly dazed and disgusted by the scene they had just witnessed, an associate producer took me aside and with great embarrassment apologized for O'Donnell's behavior. She then mentioned, somewhat sheepishly, that she had forgotten to ask me to sign the standard waiver form granting her show the right to use my appearance.

I said, "How fortuitous. If your show gets picked up and this segment gets aired, a lawyer might advise me to sue you and your show. Please fax me the form so I can consider whether I want to sign it."

It was no surprise that the fax never arrived. Lacking my signature, they could not use the segment. Since they had witnessed O'Donnell berate and falsely accuse a respected interviewee in front of a live audience, and watched a significant portion of the audience withdraw in distaste, this may have caused the producers or the network to think more carefully about the wisdom of allowing O'Donnell to host an interview show.

According to imdb.com, the Internet database for films and television programs, not only did the series never get picked up but the pilot never even aired.

I find it quite amazing that mounting evidence indicates that at least some mediums have more honesty and integrity than certain media personalities and magicians.

Who would have guessed?

Survival is in the details.
—Human Energy Systems Laboratory

8 Dead Parapsychologist Meets Live Medium

Allison provides evidence for the survival of a deceased psychic scientist's consciousness

Though Allison and other mediums are rarely perfect, the really good mediums get accurate information in all kinds of contexts—from restaurants and TV studio tapings of demonstration experiments to exploratory experiments and triple-blind studies. When I witness accurate information repeatedly obtained in so many different contexts, this kind of "cross-situational replication" provides compelling evidence that something "paranormal" is taking place.

However, as compelling as is the totality of these findings, they do not speak to the ultimate question—what is the source of the information? Of course, we don't yet know, but at present there appear to be three primary possibilities.

First, the possibility was raised earlier in these pages, that the medium may be reading the mind of the sitter. For example, when Allison first read for me, she might somehow have been reading my mind about my special friend and mentor Susy Smith.

Second, also mentioned earlier, the medium may somehow be getting the information from the "vacuum of space"—sometimes also referred to as the "zero-point field," or by contemporary physicists as the "quantum hologram," or by the term handed down from ancient Vedic Indian mystics, "Akashic Record," or by what Dr. Rupert Sheldrake, the Cambridge University-educated biologist and author of *A New Science of Life,* calls the "morphogenetic field."

Third, in theory at least, the medium might be actually receiving the information from the continued living consciousness of the person who died.

If we want to seriously entertain this last possibility, we need to ask whether we can scientifically seek an answer to the bottom-line question, "Does consciousness survive?"

Determining which of these possibilities, or some other we can't yet even guess at, is the true explanation may be one of the most challenging questions of 21st-century science.

However, if one is willing to accept this challenge, seek the evidence, and keep an open mind, surprises can and do occur that provide critical keys to answering this essential question once and for all.

As we have discussed before, surprises are the rule, not the exception, in this research. What is especially curious is that the most important surprises and evidence seem to be coming from "the other side"—as provided by sophisticated deceased scholars and scientists like the late Susy Smith, and now as well by the late British citizen Montague Keen, known to his friends as "Monty."

His widow, Veronica Keen, has taken the position of remaining in control of information regarding her late husband, and she has had the name "Montague Keen" "patented." (The term as used in England applies to this situation.) So I will here report only information that has been previously communicated publicly. What follows is a behind-the-scenes account of research that Julie Beischel (my colleague described in Chapter 6) and I conducted, and that I used in the keynote address I gave at a public tribute to Monty in London in June 2004. (A more complete scientific report was prepared for a presentation I gave at a conference on mediumship sponsored by the Parapsychology Foundation in January 2005. It was titled "Survival Is in the Details: A Double-Blind and Single-Blind Experiment." Appendix B provides an abstract of this article.

Who Was/Is Montague Keen?

Monty was, so to speak, "bigger than life," not just physically—he was a tall man—but intellectually as well. The subject matter closest to his heart was the topic of survival of consciousness after death. Monty was especially interested in the topic as evidenced by "physical mediums," who claim to be able to materialize spirits, produce voices and ectoplasm, and so forth. (For the record, that's a topic I have no direct research experience with and so take no position on, negative or positive.)

In a biography he prepared for the Internet, Monty listed himself as the principal author of the Scole Report, a 1999 study he described as "a detailed examination of the physical phenomena produced during sittings with a mediumistic group, and published by the Society for Psychical Research." He identified himself as "a lifelong member of the SPR." As a career, he served in the capacity of a Parliamentary journalist, spent 25 years as an editor specializing in agriculture, and farmed in East Anglia for over 30 years. In politics, he served as head of the Parliamentary and Legal department of the National Farmers Union of England and Wales. He was, as well, obviously proud of being "a prizeman of the Royal Agricultural College." (For more information about his pioneering research and seminal writings, see www.survivalafterdeath.org/researchers/keen.htm.)

I first met Monty in 2000 at an annual meeting of the Society for Scientific Exploration, held that year at the University of Virginia. Monty gave a talk about the Scole Report, summarizing his research with a group of physical mediums in England. I was deeply impressed with his presentation, which I found informed, organized, thorough, and challenging. Nonetheless, I had a difficult time accepting much of the evidence and his interpretations. For example, Monty claimed that the circle of physical mediums could enable spirits to imprint detailed written inscriptions on undeveloped film. (A physical medium is a person who supposedly, under the influence of a discarnate, demonstrates mind-over-matter abilities.) He claimed that fraud was not involved. I remained open-minded (I hope) but skeptical.

Monty was impressed with my laboratory's ongoing mediumship research. For a conference I co-sponsored in the spring of 2001, Monty took the long flight from London to Tucson to attend. In one session, Laurie Campbell did an informal demonstration for the audience of how we were conducting single-blind mediumship research. Since only a few people in the audience of a couple of hundred people knew who Monty was, I picked him as the secret sitter.

Over the next few years, Monty and I exchanged regular e-mails that were both serious and playful; he had a wry sense of humor. In 2003, Monty arranged for a "Study Day" (a British term for an all-day scientific conference) on the topic of survival of consciousness after death, hosted by the Society for Psychical Research. I was one of the four invited speakers; two presented evidence consistent with survival, and two presented skeptical critiques. I had the great fortune to spend almost a week with Monty and Veronica as a guest in their home, enjoying Veronica's cooking and basking in the love they had for each other.

One day in the middle of January 2004, I received a shocking e-mail from Rupert Sheldrake: Monty Keen had just dropped dead of a heart attack.

He had died, Rupert informed me, at a meeting held at the Royal Society of Arts. Rupert was the invited speaker, presenting his research on telephone telepathy. After his speech, his research had been attacked by a super-skeptic. Monty spoke up in Rupert's defense and apparently collapsed midway through a sentence. He was given CPR while the medics were en route but the efforts to save him were unsuccessful.

I later learned that the presentation had been videotaped. When I went to London that summer to participate in a special daylong tribute in Monty's honor, I had the opportunity of watching the tape of his heart attack and his ultimate death.

I was heartbroken—for Veronica, for Monty, for his family and friends, and for the work. There was only one Monty. His departure left a huge hole that no one could fill. Also, I had lost a close relationship with an elder statesperson who was both visionary role model and personal friend.

About a month later, I received a phone call from Veronica. She informed me that since Monty had died, she had been in contact with a number of mediums in England and on the Continent. Not only did these mediums claim that Monty was alive and well on the other side, but that Monty had a special request. Supposedly he wanted me to independently document in the United States that he was still here.

I had no way of knowing whether Veronica's mediums were accurately conveying Monty's wishes nor whether Veronica was interpreting them correctly. Nonetheless, I felt both a scientific and a personal obligation to give Monty's purported wishes the benefit of the doubt. It just so happened that we were conducting a new combined single-blind and double-blind mediumship study, which included a novel "asking-questions" phase. I immediately determined to add Veronica as a secret sitter.

Then, in mid-March, Veronica called me again. She informed me that she and the Society for Psychical Research would be co-hosting an all-day tribute in Monty's honor, and she asked if I would give an address. The Society's announcement of the tribute included these words:

> *He was also a prolific writer, a superb lecturer, and an indefatigable investigator, best known for his research into phenomena associated with physical mediumship. Monty died "in action" during a public debate on telepathy at the Royal Society of Arts in London on 15 January, in the middle of making a cogent point against the critics. This special meeting is being held as a tribute to Monty, in the room where he died, and will focus on those subjects to which he dedicated himself so passionately. The speakers include many of his closest collaborators and they will discuss some of his most famous cases.*

Deciding to be courageous, I chose a bold title for my keynote address: "Montague Keen's Vision of Survival of Consciousness—Then and Now." My hope was that by the time of my presentation, I might have some meaningful information to report about the "now" portion of the title.

It turned out my title was prescient.

Designing the Monty Keen Experiment

The design of the Monty readings represented a landmark in my experimental studies of the afterlife. People often ask questions such as "If mediums can really communicate with the dead, how come most of the time they get things like 'Mother loves you' or 'It wasn't your fault, I don't blame you'?" And, "If the dead can communicate, why don't you ever ask them to answer questions, such as what the afterlife is like?" In these readings, we would begin for the first time to open the door and see whether it might be possible to get responses from the other side on issues like these.

The readings, which would take place with Veronica as a sitter unidentified to the mediums and at a distant location (in England), were designed to be held in two phases. The first was double-blind, with the sitter not present during the reading and Julie serving as the "proxy sitter." The interviews with the mediums were conducted over the telephone. This phase consisted of two parts.

Part 1A was completely free form. The mediums were simply told that there was a deceased person, but they were not even given the deceased person's first name. The idea was that the deceased Susy Smith would bring the sitter's deceased loved one to the reading—the double-deceased paradigm.

In Part 1B, the mediums were typically given the first name of the sitter and were requested to ask for free form. However, because Montague's name was so unique, and because there was the remote possibility that one or more of the mediums might have known that Monty died, we decided that instead of giving the deceased person's name, we would give the mediums the widow's first name instead. For the first medium (which happened to be

Allison), the experimenter, Julie, said that the deceased was the husband of a sitter named Veronica.

Later we recognized that even this might possibly trigger an association—if a medium somehow guessed that the experiment potentially involved Monty and also knew that his wife's name was Veronica. I asked Veronica if Monty had a favorite term of endearment for her that most people would not know; she shared with me the term he was fond of using with her. With later mediums Julie said that the deceased was a husband who used to call his wife by this term of endearment.

In Part 2A, Julie asked the mediums six "life questions" concerning the deceased, such as "Give a physical description of yourself in life" and "What was your cause of death?" These questions clearly targeted specific information and could be scored for accuracy by the sitters.

Parts 2B and 2C were the crucial, groundbreaking portions of the study.

In Part 2B, Julie asked the mediums 17 "afterlife questions" concerning the deceased, such as "Where are you? Describe what it's like" and "Describe how we appear to you." These questions also targeted specific information, but of course could not be scored for accuracy. We included these questions as exploratory.

Finally, in Part 2C, Julie asked the mediums if the deceased had any comments, questions, or requests for the absent sitter.

The Phase One double-blind reading with Allison as the medium took place in the spring of 2004. The Phase Two single-blind reading with Allison as the medium occurred that summer, with Allison reading in Tucson while Julie and I were in London. For this second reading, the sitter was present and was allowed to interact with the mediums over the telephone. Our purpose was to see what additional kinds of information might be received if the sitters and mediums were allowed to interact.

As with the other readings detailed in this book, the results of the single-blind reading once again showed how dazzling the research mediums can be, and Veronica was quite impressed. She concluded that Allison was one of the very best mediums she had experienced in her years of being involved with mediums both before and after Monty's death.

Returning to the actual conduct of the Phase One experiment, when we were getting ready to have Allison perform the double-blind reading, it happened that a producer who was doing a documentary on survival research wanted to film an ongoing experiment. We decided to invite Allison to Tucson for the Phase One reading, so the reading was not conducted by Julie via telephone as we had originally planned.

Because I had a personal relationship with Monty and deeply cared about him, I wanted to include an informal, unanticipated post-double-blind-reading interview where I could ask questions of Allison regarding Monty concerning facts that I might be able to confirm.

Susy, who was being called on to help with the reading, shared with Monty many characteristics in common—including the fact that both were treated as second-class citizens by the majority of the parapsychology research community because they lacked academic credentials: neither had a Ph.D. Both did outstanding work; I don't hold much brief with those who think that no one who lacks impressive credentials can ever have anything worthwhile to offer.

Startling Transformative Findings

If you are a scientist or a skeptic (or both), you're probably most interested in the evidence from the controlled double-blind portion of the experiment; the abstract for this experiment is found in Appendix B. All I need say here is that our primary hypothesis was confirmed. We discovered that the most accurate and discriminative information was revealed during the "life questions" phase, Part 2A, in which targeted information was requested from the mediums.

Importantly, if Allison had somehow guessed that this was Monty, and knew details of his life, she would presumably have done very well during Part 1B, when she was simply given Veronica's name. The results did not support this speculation. Rather, Veronica's double-blind scoring revealed that it was the Part 2A "life questions" context that produced the statistically significant results.

Of greatest interest, though, is what happened during my subsequent questioning of Allison and what she revealed. I was quite aware that if Allison gave me information I knew to be true, she could have been just "reading my mind." Nonetheless, I wanted to know if Allison was getting anything related to Monty.

What was completely unexpected was that Monty would assert himself in the reading and reveal his apparent intentions.

Portions of the most significant parts of the reading—those that speak to the survival hypothesis in ways that seem as if they could not have been "from mind reading of the sitter" or "reading the vacuum of space"—are presented below.

The reading took place in what was then my office in the Human Energy Systems Laboratory at the University of Arizona. (The university has since provided a new, larger space for my laboratory and center near the University Hospital.) At various points in my questioning of Allison, she and I were both interrupted in totally unexpected ways. I was pressing Allison for answers to specific questions and she was trying to address those questions, but was frequently interrupted by what she experienced as the strong spirit of Monty.

Here's an example of an interruption, picking up from a point early in the session; "GS" is Gary Schwartz, "AD" is Allison DuBois, and "JB" is Julie Beischel. At this moment in my interview, I'm trying to ask a question; however, midway through the sentence, Allison cuts me off with an unrelated statement.

GS: *Can he show you any images ...*

[AD interrupts again, this time very strongly.]

AD: *He went down at a podium or ... No* [looks up and ponders]. *No* [holds her face in her hands].

GS: *What?*

AD: *Um ... he's showing a man falling at the podium. Like* [snaps her fingers]. *Like* [snaps her fingers again] *and falls, and he goes down at the podium.*

GS: *Okay.*

[I knew that Monty had died at the Royal Academy of Arts while defending Rupert Sheldrake. However, at the time of this reading, I had no idea whether there was a podium at the event or, if so, whether Monty was anywhere near it. I had no idea at this moment why Monty appeared to be interrupting. Only later, especially when I saw the videotape of his collapsing and dying, did I learn that it actually happened in front of the podium.]

AD: *Uh ... this is important. So like an assembly. And he goes down at the podium. Is that odd? That's what he's showing. The man that died at the podium.*

[This was one of the most important and clearly evidential moments in the reading. Allison had interrupted me asking a question and said, seemingly out of the blue, "He went down at a podium" at a place "like an assembly." It happened "snap"—that quickly.

GS: *Have you ever seen that before?*

AD: *No, never.*

GS: *How many readings have you done?*

AD: *Well over a thousand.*

GS: *Okay, and how often does this happen?* [AD looks pained.]

AD: *Oh ... phew. No, I don't even know what it means. He's making me feel like either he had a heart attack or* [snapping her fingers] *his breath was taken from him. But he's showing* [snap] *his knees buckling and going down.*

GS: *And he's showing you something about a podium, and a man falling down at a podium?*

AD: *Like he was talking at the podium, he was at the podium, he went down, it was the podium ... walking to the podium, or at the podium, but he went down.*

GS: *And this is important for me to know?*

AD: *Yes* [looks confused]. *There's an acknowledgement of this man being important.*

[I knew that Monty had died suddenly, of a heart attack, at an "assembly." I had been informed that Monty and Veronica had sat in the front row. However, as I mentioned above, I did not know at the time of the reading that there was a podium at the meeting and that the two speakers spoke at or near the podium. Allison was incorrect in saying he went down "at" the podium, which she said twice, in saying he went down "at" the podium, which she said twice, and when she said he was "walking to the podium," which was also incorrect. And Allison was emphatic that the deceased was saying that this information was important for me.]

GS: *Okay. So this is a way of answering the question that I would know that it's him?*

AD: *Yes.* [She is confused and laughs.]

GS: *And you don't know what's going on?*

AD: *No ....*

GS: *It's very important that this be recorded.*

JB: *So he wanted to tell Veronica about the curtains* [mentioned earlier in the reading] ...

GS: *Right.*

JB: *And Gary about the man at the podium?*

GS: *Right. About the heart attack and falling down or something.*

[Allison was clearly confused about this. She had never experienced such a death scene before—a man who had dropped dead of a heart attack at an assembly involving a podium. She felt as if she was being pressed by the deceased to communicate this information.]

AD: *And he's referencing this being a very nice man.*

GS: *Who's a very nice man?*

AD: *The one that went down at the podium.*

GS: *Ah ha. The one that went down at the podium was a nice man. And did I know this person was a nice man?*

AD: *Yes.*

[Monty was, indeed, a very nice man. Obviously Allison was getting accurate information. Much of this information I knew ahead of time, so I knew that she was making accurate statements about the unidentified deceased person, Monty. However, I did not know anything about a podium, nor was I prepared for this information to be insistently conveyed, over and over, by the deceased. Clearly, Allison was not reading my mind about this. And it is not an attribute of "dead information" to insist on being communicated, to the point of interrupting the session.]

Interruptions continued. Here's another one:

GS: *Okay. Is there anything else …*

[AD interrupts.]

AD: *He's referencing e-mails. Like he sent you e-mails or people affiliated with him sent you the e-mails but he's referencing the e-mails being sent.*

GS: *What about them?*

AD: *Um … ahh … a "thorn in the side." Like the thorn in the side. Like it was to provoke or there was some firing back and forth.*

GS: *And was he playing this role, or was someone else playing this role?*

AD: *It feels like people connected to him played this role. He may have played this role, but he is referencing him being on the other end of the computer from you.*

GS: *Okay.*

AD: And this message is being sent.

GS: *And how would I know that this was him? I mean, a lot of people send me e-mails!*

AD: *Because he says that nobody forgets his e-mails!*

[Everybody laughs.]

GS: *Yes, but he has to tell you something besides the "thorn in the side"—which is pretty good by the way—that's really pretty good.*

AD: *Um … He also says … like you'll elaborate on some things, and he is more of "short and sweet" or um … "a burst of comments" … and you elaborate academically and he's got all the knowledge in his head that he had and was just repeating what he'd known. He's just repeating it. Not that he knew that he believed it, but repeating it.*

GS: *Ah ... so you are saying that he had less conviction about even the things that he was writing about?*

AD: *Um ... he needed to believe that what he was writing about was the case because if it wasn't then he had no understanding of what life really was.*

GS: *Oh ... okay.*

AD: *And he says like, "Shake a stick at you." I don't know what the old expression is, but he's showing like shaking a stick at you.*

GS: *Okay.*

Allison had no knowledge that I was in e-mail contact with the deceased for the past five years. She did not know that Monty played the role of being a "thorn in the side" as a wonderful critic not only of the severe skeptics but of the active researchers in the field as well—including me and my team—and in the role of supporter and critic even served on Julie's international advisory committee for her postdoctoral fellowship. Monty did write "short and sweet" e-mails as well as "bursts of comments" that were erudite and challenging.

He was ambivalent about "mental" mediumship—the kind that Allison and the other mediums discussed in this book do. Though he very much wanted to believe, he still had serious questions about what conclusions could be drawn from the mediumship research to date. And he did at various times "shake a stick" at me. It has been my experience that people who are "bigger than life" in life tend to appear "bigger than life" in the afterlife.

According to Veronica, after he passed, at least one medium spontaneously told her that Monty was continuing to "shake a stick" at me. That's especially meaningful in the context of this particular research reading.

As you can probably guess, experiencing these interruptions, accompanied by the specific information, was meaningful.

Imagine that you question the existence of ducks. There's that old saying about when something looks like a duck, walks like a duck, quacks like a duck, and so forth, it probably is a duck. The persistent appearance of interruptions in the face of questions by the experimenter—me—was an example of Monty acting like a duck with a mind of its own.

I want to provide one more example of Monty's interruptions, one that I think is quite profound.

GS: *What does he think about you? Is he pleased with what you've done to date?*

AD: *Uh, yes.*

GS: *He is?*

AD: *He is.*

GS: *And can he ...*

[AD interrupts.]

AD: *He's showing the "white crow" as being important. And to go back to the white crow.*

GS: *[in disbelief] What?*

[AD and JB laugh.]

GS: *This is really great. Keep going. What are you saying? This is really important.*

AD: *Like the "white crow" experiment was important or "go back to the white crow experiment" or the white crow.*

GS: *And he is saying that this is like a white crow?*

AD: [sounding unsure] *I guess. I don't know if he is saying that, but he is saying, "Go back to the white crow" or that the white crow is important. He is showing the white crow as being connected.*

GS: *Isn't that interesting? Do you have any idea what he's referring to?*

AD: *I know an experiment was done by that name. I don't know what the experiment is.*

GS: *Do you know what it means?*

AD: *No. I have no idea what a white crow is ...*

GS: *Okay.*

AD: *... because I've never seen one.*

GS: *You have never seen a white crow? So you don't even know its symbolism?*

AD: *No.*

GS: *You don't remember its symbolism or whatever?*

AD: *No.*

GS: *And you don't know why he's bringing it up at this moment?*

AD: *That was before I came into the picture [meaning "before I started working with you"], so I don't know.*

JB: *You just know it as the name of the experiment.*

AD: *Right.*

GS: *And he's saying that this applies to you?*

AD: *Uh . . . I . . . I . . . I don't know. He's just mentioning the white crow.*

GS: *I got ya, but, see, I asked the question, "What does he think about you, what does he think about what's happening here?" and you're saying this is "white crow." So that becomes meaningful. And he would know that if this was him.*

AD: *Ah. Well, I would rather be a white crow than a black crow.*

JB: *You are.*

GS: *Yes, trust me, you would really rather be.*

[Everyone laughs.]

GS: *This period of time is definitely "white crow material."*

Skeptics often reject the conclusion that a medium is acquiring information using paranormal means by concluding that he or she is using visual or auditory clues to "cold read" a sitter. As mentioned above, as with most other experiments performed in our laboratory, this experiment included a double-blind phase to eliminate this possibility. In the informal post-double-blind experimental session described here, Allison is involved in an open dialogue with me yet she still remains objective in her descriptions, even when encouraged to interpret the statements she is making. Allison is tough, and this is to her credit.

For example, when I asked her if the "white crow" symbol applies to her, Allison continued to report that the deceased was simply mentioning the white crow. As I stated during the reading, Allison does not allow people to put words into her mouth, nor does she adopt interpretations offered to her by someone else.

This was also demonstrated earlier in the reading, when Allison was not influenced by my "trick question" about the deceased's education. I had asked Allison a question implying that Monty had a Ph.D.: "Can you get any sense about his education?" Allison's response was novel and hesitant; I had never in a research reading heard this kind of reply: "You want to go someplace that he kind of is hesitant to even go is the way he is putting it .... He thinks you know that it's him." Allison was correct; it sure sounded like him.

Of course, we cannot ever be certain what is in someone else's heart or mind; we can rarely be certain when another person is being absolutely truthful. Yet in all my extensive work with Allison, I have seen a dedication to honesty and no effort at all to make things come out the way someone else wants them to. I am convinced she truly did not understand the metaphorical meaning of "white crow," as explained earlier in these pages. Yet the phrase represented a huge compliment. And unless Allison was pulling the wool over my eyes, it was a huge compliment coming from Montague Keen.

Survival Is in the Details

As we have seen, evidence for survival requires more than just accurate information from mediums. The information must "behave" in a way that fits the criteria of "living." The information must behave as if it has a "life of its own." It's not just to be received and read. It is not "passive." It is as persistent and complicated and contradictory and playful as the consciousness that apparently generates it. I say "apparently" because scientifically it is virtually impossible to prove that anyone is conscious—not even the living, much less the deceased.

If I talk with you in person or on the telephone, I do not experience your consciousness directly. I see you behave (if we are face to face) or I just hear you (if we are on the telephone). That is what I experience and measure. I then "infer" that you are conscious, because you behave in a way that is consistent with what I understand as consciousness, based upon my own experience. The truth is, the only consciousness that I know for sure exists is my own consciousness (and sometimes I question that—being, as I've said, a well-trained orthodox agnostic).

The information from Monty's reading obviously does not prove survival of consciousness. However, it's strongly consistent with it.

In scientific papers, we speak of the "discarnate intention" hypothesis—scientific jargon for "spirit intention." There are various ways that discarnates/spirits/the deceased can show us that they have intention. No one of these ways constitutes proof, but together they provide a very strong case.

The deceased can "drop in" unannounced and even uninvited. If they show up with a purpose, this implies intention. We have witnessed many instances of "drop-ins" in our research.

The deceased can interrupt the sitter, experimenter, and medium. In the reading just related, as you've read, this happened propitiously and repeatedly.

The deceased can provide evidence for what is termed "cross-correspondence." This is where different mediums receive different information, but the information does not make sense until all the separate pieces are brought together and combined. From my experience, it appears to take a highly intelligent and sophisticated discarnate to coordinate such activities. Monty was especially interested in cross-correspondence. Though beyond the scope of this chapter, evidence of both between-medium cross-correspondence and within-reading cross-correspondence showed up in the Monty reading.

The deceased can also selectively withhold information. This is very clever. One instance of this concerned my trick question regarding Monty's education and his apparent cryptic response that only he would know I would be able to interpret.

Once we give the deceased the benefit of the doubt—meaning, we make the assumption that they are really present—numerous possibilities arise for them to establish that they are here, as conscious intentional "beings" (or energies, spirits, souls, etc.). However, we have to be open to seeing the evidence.

The phrase "survival is in the details" speaks to this fundamental truth. If we provide only summary graphs of double-blind and triple-blind experiments, give means and standard deviations of the numbers, and provide statistics and p values, we will miss the bottom-line evidence that distinguishes among the three paranormal hypotheses—mind reading of the sitter, reading information from the vacuum of space or other so-called "super psi" explanations, and survival.

Theoretically, all three phenomena may be real. It may not be an either-or choice. In fact, there is scientific evidence consistent with all three possibilities—a subject for another book. Our focus is on whether mediums can indeed speak with the deceased.

Thanks to Allison's gifts, plus Monty's apparent continued commitment to the work, the evidence points strongly in the direction of Monty and Susy, and by extension all of our loved ones, continuing their consciousness like the light from distance stars.

The question is, are we prepared to listen?

> *Ye shall know the truth, and the truth shall make you mad.*
>
> *—Aldous Huxley*

9 Skeptics: Fact and Fantasy

Why professional skeptics say Allison and other mediums are committing fraud—when they are not

A distinguished parapsychologist, Professor Charles Tart—known to his friends as Charlie—once gave me a heart-warming pep talk (more precisely, a pep e-mail) after I had been vigorously and viciously attacked by James Randi, one of the most vocal professional skeptics. Sometimes known by his stage-magician name of "The Amazing Randi," he has claimed publicly, in writing—based only on his assumptions and prejudices, without offering a single piece of evidence—that I have been readily fooled by deceptive mediums. Worse, he has implied that I might be cheating.

Charlie's comment was along these lines: "If the only criticism that can be raised about a given experiment to explain the findings is that the experimenter must have somehow been cheating, then the experimenter knows that he has designed a really good experiment."

I am perpetually wary of anyone approaching the laboratory with extraordinary claims. My wariness does not apply simply to purported mediums and psychics, but it even extends to people claiming to be interested in funding our research as well. I have sadly learned that I must keep my guard up about everyone if I am to protect the integrity of the work.

We take our motto seriously: "If it is real, it will be revealed; and if it is fake, we'll find the mistake." This includes always being on the lookout for frauds and cheats. Our responsibility is to defend the truth—be it standing up for a person who has a genuine gift or exposing someone who is faking a gift. Because my colleagues and I are overt about our intentions, and we design our studies so carefully, even professional mental magicians who are also skeptics refuse to participate in our research—knowing their tricks will not work under the conditions of our experiments. For example, when we caught a 17-year-old woman engaging in subtle cheating in research, we stopped the experiment and published our efforts uncovering her deception in a paper in the *Journal of Scientific Exploration*.

Randi once planted two trained magicians in a parapsychology laboratory at a major university. His "secret agents" presented themselves as individuals claiming to have psychic abilities. He hoped to demonstrate that scientists could be fooled into concluding that a given person was psychic when in fact the person was using tricks from the magician's repertoire. The laboratory was appropriately embarrassed, their funding was ended, and the laboratory eventually closed.

Randi made his point—and it was a good one. If a given scientist could be fooled, then her or his data could be suspect. What Randi apparently fails to realize is that he made his point three decades ago, and that most sophisticated researchers working in frontier science today appreciate the dangers of fraud and trickery, and design their experiments with every conceivable precaution to protect against fraud and deception.

If history continues, the Randis of the world who read these pages will brashly conclude that the findings I have reported must be due to ineptitude, if not fraud, on the part of the mediums or sitters, and, even worse, the experimenters. Can we trust their conclusions?

Evolution of Knowledge through Research Rather than Ridicule

History reminds us that humankind's collective knowledge continually grows and evolves through the process of scientific exploration and research. For example, at one time the best scientists in the world accepted the "truth" that the atom was the smallest particle of matter. Research subsequently revealed that atoms are made up of a nucleus with electrons swirling around it. Still later, quantum physicists described the electrons swirling around the nucleus as having properties like "clouds," "waves," and "probabilities." We now know that even these are not the smallest particles and waves in nature; new sub-atomic particles continue to be discovered, and currently physics is theorizing about super-miniature waves—"superstrings"—as potentially being the fundamental building blocks of nature.

Similarly, when ideas such as "black holes" and "dark energy" in the universe were first offered, they sounded like fanciful science fiction, yet eventually turned out to be supported by new evidence.

In the same way, one aspect of Randi's claims may eventually turn out to be true. Just as further discoveries revealed that the atom is not the basic building block of nature, further discoveries might reveal some other, more fundamental explanation for what the mediums are able to do. The history of science reminds us to remain open—with humility—to potential new discoveries that will be revealed through future experimentation.

My working hypothesis, offered with humility, can be expressed in the form of an analogy:

> *Survival of consciousness theory may be to psychology as superstring theory is to physics—the most fundamental of explanations.*

Future research will tell.

My point is this: new scientific understandings don't come about because people like Randi ridicule the scientists, researchers, and innovative thinkers. They come about because scientists conduct experiments that lead to new discoveries, new understandings, or new theories, and other scientists test the new work, eventually either supporting it or refuting it. If Randi thinks my work with mediums is flawed, he is welcome to do new research, or fund new research, to test the findings, and to publish his results in scientific journals and books, as my colleagues and I have published ours.

We advance our understanding of the universe through research, not through ridicule. Randi's attacks, until they are backed up by scientific evidence, only make him look foolish.

For the record, I thank Randi for his sometimes honest efforts at protecting the public from fraud and pseudo-science, but I do not condone his dishonest efforts to prevent the public from seeing the research when the information disagrees with his blatant biases.

My intention here is not to pick on Randi. I am sharing with you some of my experiences with him because they are enlightening. They illustrate some of the devious ploys used by the professional, high-profile skeptics.

Randi would have you believe I claim (I'm quoting Randi directly) that "the university has scientifically-derived evidence proving that certain people can actually converse with those who are dead."

It is not the university doing this work, but my colleagues and I. More to the point, I don't claim, and never have that "certain people can actually converse with those who are dead." I have simply reported that replicated evidence under controlled conditions has been gathered in my laboratory—and recently in Scotland by Professor Emeritus Archie Roy and Tricia Robertson—indicating that some individuals can obtain accurate information regarding the deceased. I have stated that the evidence *appears to strongly suggest* that they are somehow obtaining information from the deceased, but no reputable scientist would jump from the evidence currently available to assert such a conclusion definitively.

So Randi, in his rabid eagerness to hold on to the notion that there is no continuation of consciousness after death, misstates the conclusions and remains blind and closed-minded to the possibilities. He lives, in other words, in the same camp as those who forced Galileo to recant his claims that the earth revolves around the sun. Randi possesses a closed, 17th-century mind in a 21st-century world.

In April 2005, with a laugh, I wrote a memo responding to a letter he had addressed to Richard Imwalle, President of the University of Arizona Foundation. Why the laugh? Because the man had made an outlandish promise which, for reasons you will quickly understand, he has failed to keep. But as I wrote I pictured him in the act.

This skeptic has established a prize for anyone who can provide acceptable evidence for any paranormal phenomena, including that communication with the dead is possible, and he loves bragging to the press that no one—including me—has ever attempted to collect the reward for mediumship. What he doesn't mention is the condition for collecting: evidence submitted will be examined by a panel he himself has appointed; he calls it an "Independent Qualified Panel," but it is composed mostly of people hand-picked to guarantee that the decision would likely be a forgone conclusion, merely rubber-stamping his prejudices.

But even about this, the man has been patently dishonest. His letter to Mr. Imwalle named Dr. Stanley Krippner as one of the members of his panel. Dr. Krippner, a professor of psychology at Saybrook Graduate School and Research Center, San Francisco, is a Fellow in three divisions of the American Psychological Association, and former president of two divisions. To put it in layman's terms, he is an esteemed psychologist. And he was certainly highly acceptable to me. I felt reassured that Randi would have so highly regarded a scientist on his panel.

However, there was, it turned out, a small problem. Dr. Krippner advised me that he had been contacted by Randi, but that he had declined to serve on this proposed committee. He had, he advised me, told Randi that he would *not* agree to serve on such a committee. Yet here was Randi claiming him as a committee member.

I did not wish to embarrass Randi, so I kept this issue (and others) out of the public eye. However, I did share privately with a few personal contacts who questioned me about this that Dr. Krippner had clearly not agreed to serve on Randi's panel. One of my contacts, Pam Blizzard, was sufficiently incensed by Randi's behavior that she e-mailed him about it.

Randi was not happy. On May 11, 2001, he responded by posting on the Internet, "If Pam Blizzard—whoever she is—said that, either she is a blatant liar or Schwartz has misrepresented the situation. I very much doubt that Schwartz e-mailed that to Pam. All four of those persons have agreed to be listed and to serve on the committee."

His Internet posting continued, "Here's a challenge: If Pam Blizzard will identify this proposed person—who I notice is not named!—and provide the statement in which he said that if he had been contacted by me and asked to serve, he would have declined, I'll push a peanut across Times Square with my nose, naked. How can she pass up *that* offer?"

I contacted Dr. Krippner and asked him if I could share his e-mail to me stating the truth. He agreed. I shared this information with Pam. She passed this on to Randi. Did Randi honor his public challenge and "Push a peanut across Times Square with his nose, naked"? No. What he did was ignore the fact that he made this commitment.

Randi further wrote on the Internet, "What's your response, Pam? Who is it, and where's the evidence? Derived from Tarot cards? Or just a plain old LIE?"

Pam sent Randi the evidence. It did not come from Tarot cards; it came from Dr. Krippner.

Whom Are We to Believe?

Whom are we to believe? Who is telling the truth?

Most professional skeptics are skilled in rhetoric. They are facile in writing and speaking. They can even be endearing at times. The media typically seeks them out whenever some extraordinary claim is made. And we, the public—and yes, I include myself as a member of the public—read the newspapers and magazines, listen to the radio interviews, and see the TV shows. Most of the time, we trust that the visible media skeptics are providing fair and honest criticism.

Sometimes they are telling the truth, at least as far as I can perceive. But unfortunately this is not always so. Sometimes they twist the facts, sidestep the issues, throw up smoke screens, and use other techniques of chicanery to obfuscate the truth. I have experienced their deceptive side firsthand on numerous occasions. At some point, this has to stop. The commitment throughout the media needs to meet the standard offered by Pat Mitchell, the CEO of the Public Broadcasting System, "to pursue the truth without regard for the consequences."

My extensive research experience with Allison DuBois and other gifted mediums is that by and large their mediumship motives are pure—they genuinely believe they have these gifts for a higher purpose: to serve humanity, as well as serving their personal concept of divinity. This does not mean that the mediums I have worked with are perfect human beings, nor that they do not make mistakes, nor that they do not sometimes get swept up in the excitement of celebrity attention. On balance, their purpose is to convey the truth about mediumship and what they do.

A wise critic will point out the weaknesses and limitations in each of the informal and formal experiments I have reported in this book, and critics are correct to do so. Our research team pays close attention to the details, including the limitations. My purpose here has not been to selectively present the "best" experiments from a methodological point of view, but to share with you the breadth and depth of observations I have made about Allison DuBois, peppered with examples from other mediums, so that you can come to your own conclusion about the reality of Allison's mediumship skills.

I suspect Randi does not realize it, but his flamboyant and duplicitous behavior helps to highlight a larger issue here—the question of what is more important: supporting our biases or discovering the truth?

What is more important—clever entertainment ... or genuine education?

What is more important—sophisticated hypocrisy ... or straightforward honesty?

Who are the ultimate deceivers—the dedicated mediums ... or the attacking skeptics so convinced of their own infallibility that they will not examine the evidence?

There is more hunger for love and appreciation in this world than for bread.
—Mother Teresa

10 The Meaning for All of Us, Including the Mediums

If mediumship is real, what implications does this have for how humanity will foster love, take responsibility for our relationships and environment, and celebrate the mystery—and magnificence—of the universe?

What does it mean if the findings described in this book are real—that at least some mediums are in fact actually able to communicate with the dead? What if Allison DuBois is a real medium? What if the three waves of mediums who have worked in my laboratory are all real? (Wave I included John Edward, Suzane Northrop, Anne Gehman, and Laurie Campbell; Wave II included Laurie Campbell, Allison DuBois, Mary Occhino, and Janet Mayer; Wave III included Janet Mayer, Debbie Martin, Traci Bray, and Doreen Molloy.)

What are these mediums explicitly and implicitly teaching us? Are we—all of us, non-mediums and mediums alike—ready to listen and learn? Are we prepared to wake up and grow? Are we mature and wise enough to celebrate the positive implications joyfully, and handle the negative implications carefully?

Because in addition to the positive implications of this work, there are negative ones as well. If we are to honor the totality of the truth, we must speak of these things—positive and negative. We must face them squarely and respond appropriately.

I'm listing them here as lessons—some of the lessons I've learned in the process of doing this work. I'd like to think this might lead you to ponder what all this could mean for you and your loved ones.

So, let's accept for the moment that mediumship is real, and see what some of the implications would be if that were true.

Lesson 1: *It Takes Bravery to Be a Genuine Medium (or Believe That Mediums Can Be Genuine), and This Has Its Costs.* Being a genuine medium, even a research medium, is not easy. Some of the mediums I've worked with have written about this in their books. I recounted in *The Afterlife Experiments* something that John Edward shared with me that wrenched my heart and is worth repeating here.

John wrote me one day in an e-mail that he was tired of being perceived as a "freak." I responded with a question, here paraphrased: "What would you rather be called, a freak or a fraud?" Talk about being between a rock and a hard place!

The truth is that it personally hurts genuine mediums to be called either freaks or frauds. What genuine mediums would rather be called are "humanity's friends"—whose purpose is to serve our loved ones who have passed on as well as we who are grieving them. The mediums would like us to see them as serving our souls as well as the souls of those who have "crossed over." The genuine mediums wish their true intentions to be known—that their purpose is beneficent, and that they can help humanity face its greatest challenges if we are willing to let them.

Imagine that you are a genuine medium. How would you feel if people said that you were crazy, or that you were taking advantage of grieving parents, spouses, and children, or even that you were doing the work of the devil? What would you tell people when you went to dinner, or you were on an airplane, and someone asked you, "What do you do?" Which is easier to explain to people, that you are a psychic medium, or that you are, for example, a professional skeptic?

Being a medium is not easy. Mediums typically learn to be guarded, some very much so. Some of their personal wounds, and their personal challenges and problems, stem from this constant exposure to dismissal, if not ridicule. Unless the medium has the strength of a John Edward or an Allison DuBois, he or she is not about to stand up in public and say, "I see dead people" or even "I hear dead people."

(Parenthetically, being a researcher who investigates the truth about mediums is not easy either. In most areas of science, positive findings are viewed in a positive manner—the findings are enjoyed and appreciated by other scientists, and occasionally by non-scientists as well. However, in certain areas of science, such as mediumship research, positive findings make some people—from skeptics to fundamentalists—experience significant distress, if not fury. These individuals view researchers working in such areas as being frauds or fools, if not actually doing "science on behalf of the devil.")

Finally, bereaved persons who seek out a medium often find themselves ostracized or at least criticized by family members. I have heard countless painful stories of people labeled "the black sheep of the family" because they went to a medium after a loved one died. Certain members of their families, as well as some of their friends, judged them as being naïve, gullible, weird, if not crazy for seeking the assistance of a medium. Not only do many people who have consulted mediums feel it is unsafe to share their direct personal experiences of deceased loved ones, but they feel it is necessary to hide the evidence they may have received through the medium, even through a reputable one.

Hopefully someday society will be transformed. Imagine that research continues to be conducted and that the evidence points inexorably to the reality of mediumship and survival of consciousness after death. Imagine that tomorrow's children grow up knowing, scientifically, that there is a larger spiritual reality and that they too have the potential to develop their mediumship skills and even become professional mediums if they so choose. One side effect, I hope, would be that tomorrow's mediums would not endure the scorn and pain that led them at one time to being burned at the stake, and today can lead to them being figuratively burned by the skeptics of our society and the skeptics of the media.

Lesson 2: *It's Mostly About Love—But There Is Danger Here Too.* Why do most people seek out mediums? The answer is simple—they have lost someone they loved, and they want to know that their loved one is OK or want to continue to be in contact, especially if the deceased is a child. And often, too, there's a desire to resolve certain issues with their beloved—a form of therapy between "here" and "there."

Probably my greatest inspiration has come from parents who have lost children. Some of these parents have become close friends, such as Phran and Bob Ginsberg. A few years ago, their youngest daughter, Bailey, was in an auto accident not far from their house. Bailey was killed; her older brother almost died. Losing a child you love is one of the most painful of life's experiences, and even worse, I believe, when it's unexpected.

Phran and Bob experienced great grief, but Phran, the more spiritual of the two, was open to the idea of survival of consciousness. Bob was more skeptical; he had been raised, like me, to believe it was "ashes to ashes, dust to dust, case closed."

However, they read *The Afterlife Experiments*, and it opened their eyes to the possibility not only that survival might be real, but that they could validate this for themselves. They went on a quest, had readings with multiple mediums, and examined the accuracy of each medium following guidelines described in my book. After their reading with Laurie Campbell, Bob felt compelled to call me and in time I was able to speak with him. Phran and Bob became involved in our research. One thing led to another, and the Ginsbergs decided that something must be done to allow other parents to have the healing experiences they had through afterlife science.

They created Forever Family Foundation. I serve as honorary president, but the work of the foundation is wholly theirs and that of the team of families who work with them. Not only are they helping parents, but they are setting standards for responsible, evidence-based mediums and they are making new discoveries in the context of their personal experiences. One of their goals is to help foster future research. (See www.foreverfamilyfoundation.org.)

What motivates Phran and Bob? First and foremost, it is love. It is their love for Bailey, and the evidence from research mediums that Bailey loves them, that sets the stage for everything else. And it is their commitment to science and truth that propels them.

If love is like the light from distant stars, which continues long after the stars have "died," then love takes on a much deeper, more permanent meaning and purpose. However, if the energy of love can continue, so too can the energy of hate. The fact is, the energies continue, too, of those people who have been neglected and abused. Just as the energies/spirits of Mother Teresa and Princess Diana continue, so to do the energies of Hitler and Jack the Ripper. There is a risk in "opening one's channels to spirits." As society becomes open to the reality of spirits, the downside is that "negative spirits" may have an increased freedom to influence the world.

History shows us that the science fiction of today sometimes becomes the science of tomorrow. Creative and visionary novelists and screenwriters sometimes show us in their fiction where society and science may be headed. Movies where the spirits are portrayed in a positive light, such as *Ghost* (which includes a humorous scene where a fake medium, played by Whoopi Goldberg, discovers she is actually receiving communication from a dead man, played by Patrick Swayze) and *Dragonfly,* are balanced by movies where the spirits are shown as negative, including comedies such as *Ghost Busters* (a farce involving parapsychologists played by Bill Murray, Dan Aykroyd, and Harold Ramis, with obvious negative overtones about evil ghosts and spirits) and sci-fi movies such as *White Noise* (about the potential dangerous consequences of purported electronic voice communication). Inspiring fantasies brought to life in movies like *Field of Dreams* are balanced by dark movies like *The Devil's Advocate*.

If mediums are correct, and survival of consciousness is real, then the truth is that we must consider in the equation not just the continuance of love but also the continuance of hate. I suspect that one of the major reasons why certain people, especially professional skeptics, are so fanatically against the potential reality of survival of consciousness is that they unconsciously recognize, and fear, the double-edged sword provided by genuine mediums.

Lesson 3: *Help Is Available if We're Willing to Ask for It.* Apparently there are certain advantages to shedding one's body. For example, communications that appear to come from the deceased tell us that it's easier to get around. One can supposedly travel at the speed of thought. It's much easier to multitask "on the other side." It has been claimed one can even be in more than one place at the same time. Whereas I can imagine right now that I am in Taos, New Mexico, exploring my favorite Native American pueblo, I am physically in Tucson, Arizona, typing on my keyboard. However, supposedly after I die, I can functionally be both in Taos and Tucson at the same time. I can imagine certain benefits to having that ability.

Also, it has been claimed that "on the other side" one can gain a broader perspective to what is happening "here" in the physical world. It's possible to see the bigger picture, and also see more clearly into the future.

Many mediums claim, usually off the record, that they receive information from distinguished scientists, artists, religious leaders, and politicians. Laurie Campbell is up-front about claiming that she regularly receives communication from Sir James Clerk Maxwell, the father of electromagnetic theory, as well as from the rock star Freddie Mercury of Queen. I know at least five mediums who claim they often receive communication from Albert Einstein. The fact is, if mediums can hear from your deceased mother or son, theoretically they can hear from Mother Teresa or Mahatma Gandhi as well. Energy is energy; spirit is spirit.

Why would we want to be in communication with the late Susy Smith, the late Professor John Mack of Harvard, the late Dr. Martin Luther King Jr., or the late Dr. Emanuel Swedenborg? I have deliberately listed four individuals, two I knew personally (Susy and John) and two I did not know but whose ideas I value (Dr. King and

Dr. Swedenborg), to illustrate a point. If individuals "on the other side" who are intelligent, wise, and caring can potentially help us address the critical challenges we face as a species—personally, politically, environmentally, spiritually—shouldn't we seek their help? Isn't it time to give these sophisticated and caring people the opportunity to assist us in our evolving in the physical?

If we can find a source of intuition and inspiration in the physical in those who have "crossed over" before us, would it not be in our best interest to foster receiving such counsel? Of course, in the process of seeking advice (from people here or those who have crossed over), one must be careful both to select the right advisors and to be sure to receive accurately what they are communicating.

If ever there was a need for humanity to seek help in solving its pressing problems, it is now. Research mediums, appropriately trained and tested, could perhaps serve us by making it possible to bring forth essential wisdom and guidance.

Lesson 4: *Mediums, Scientists, and Society Need to Evolve Together.* Presuming that survival of consciousness is real, there is a pressing need for all of us to grow—mediums, scientists, and the public at large. This includes each of us shedding certain things we have been taught by our parents, teachers, and religious leaders, and transforming our minds, behaviors, and institutions accordingly.

Mediums need to become more science-minded and scientists need to be more survival-minded. Although highly visible mediums like John Edward and Allison Dubois, and less visible but equally talented mediums like Laurie Campbell and Mary Occhino, have made substantial historic contributions to research on the reality and nature of mediumship, there is much more that can be—and must be—done if mediumship is to become accepted, scientifically and ethically, by mainstream society.

The Human Energy Systems Laboratory has created a new set of guidelines for what we are calling "integrative research mediums." This new wave of mediums is being educated in the history of research on mediumship, and we are treating them as collaborators rather than as subjects. We are requiring that they take the

University of Rochester Human Subjects Protection Program research ethics examination, which is regularly required in scientific programs of all investigators, including research assistants and research healers, who interact with human subjects and their data. We are encouraging established research mediums to serve as mentors for new mediums and to foster increased professional standards and ethics.

Conversely, scientists need to become more survival-minded. Rather than dismissing the possibility of survival of consciousness as a foolish superstition inconsistent with conventional neuroscience, survival-minded scientists need to recognize what Professor William James, Dr. Wilder Penfield, and Sir John Eccles—three preeminent scientists of the 20th century—understood and published. It turns out that all of the findings in contemporary neuroscience are actually consistent with the hypothesis that the brain serves as an "antenna-receiver" for consciousness rather than being the "creator" of consciousness. This does not underscore the importance of the brain; it views the brain as having a different function in the realm of mind and consciousness.

All of us can be helped to a better life if we become more survival-minded. If we knew that our very essence—our conscious awareness, including our memories, preferences, desires, and dreams—continued after we died, we would experience our current physical lives in a larger context. We would not have to experience everything, or have everything, in this lifetime. We would recognize that what we learned here, and the relationships we cultivated, would continue. We would realize that we could not avoid facing the pain and suffering we caused others. The ancient Eastern idea of Karma takes on new meaning when we view life in a survival-minded way.

Can our textbooks, professors, religious institutions, clergy, political organizations, and governmental leaders change accordingly? The history of science and society says yes. It's worth remembering there was a time when humanity believed that the earth was flat, that the sun revolved around the earth, that objects were solid, that information disappeared in the vacuum of space. We are poised to change our minds and beliefs again. Our ability to survive and evolve depends upon it.

Lesson 5: *The Future Is in the Children.* At first glance, this sounds like a cliché; stay with me.

I have met some remarkable young children and teenagers, especially those whose mothers happen to be mediums. Not only do many of them seem to have the gift, but they are growing up in homes where the gift is simply part of the household. It is possible that children today are developing these gifts in increasing numbers.

Children today take cell phones and global communication for granted. They assume that anything that they can imagine can be manifested on a computer screen or a movie screen. They are growing up watching cartoons of transformation with powerful beings, skilled not simply with super weapons, but also with super morals. They see the mess we are making of our environment, more so than any previous generation. Young people in advanced modern societies are becoming sensitive enough, and brave enough, to envision changing the whole world.

Yes, many children today are deprived of loving and stable homes. And yes, many are exposed to early sex and drugs. But others are seeing the power of creative minds and caring hearts, and are not afraid to have big dreams. Labels like "indigo" (as used in the book *The Indigo Children*) are scientifically questionable, but some sort of transformation is taking place in at least a subset of children.

Think about this. Millions of mothers and their children are watching NBC's *Medium*, and soon millions more will be watching other shows ready to capitalize on NBC's success. The fact that *Medium* is mostly entertainment rather than based on actual experiences is less important than the fact that it is appearing at this moment in history.

If the afterlife research continues to be positive, if funding emerges to make it possible for other researchers to replicate and extend what we are doing, if the media continues to expand its coverage of the power of the human mind to connect with and be part of a larger spiritual reality, who knows what potentials will be manifest in the next generation of children? The future of our species, if not this planet, is ultimately in their hands. They are humanity's hope and opportunity.

The Truth about *Medium* and the Future of Psychic Entertainment

There is a time and place for fiction. I enjoy reading good mysteries, for example, that are carefully crafted and well written. I read them partly for fun, and yes, partly for escape (even escape from medium research). I like to take a vacation with my mind, so to speak. Often when I travel, I will read a mystery—be it a detective story or a science fiction story—depending upon what is available at the airport bookstore.

However, when I read such a book, I know it is fiction. Even if the novel is inspired by real life, I know that the writer has felt free to serve more as storyteller than educator, creating a book that is focused more on entertainment than edification.

It distresses me that so many people who watch programs like *Medium* cannot tell what is real and what is made up. An acquaintance recently mentioned the series, and I asked him quite innocently how much of the show he thought was real. His response surprised me. He said, quite seriously, "Almost a hundred percent."

Does this matter?

Another recent conversation about the show was with my brother. I reminded him that we had exchanged e-mails months earlier about the *Medium* story involving a university professor similar to me, and the professor's missing brother. As discussed in the introduction of this book, I tried to help my brother understand that while I had found the episode well done and entertaining, *Medium* is a dramatic series, which means that the writers can take liberties with the facts and even make up entire stories.

He then told me in our phone conversation that after I had e-mailed him explaining that much of the current stories were fiction, he and his wife had stopped watching the series. He explained that once he knew that much of the show was entertainment, it no longer held his interest. As long as he thought the stories were based on real events, he watched the show, partly because he thought it might help him understand this aspect of my work, but more importantly because he thought it might help him come to his own conclusion about the reality of mediums and survival of consciousness after death.

At first I was surprised by my brother's attitude. However, it's not difficult to understand his reasoning and feelings. The Website of the NBC network describes *Medium* as being "a drama series ... inspired by" Allison, which is far different than claiming all the stories and events are true. On the other hand, my brother's thirst to know what is real about such a profound psychological and spiritual question, and his comment to me that he hopes new series will emerge that show what really happens with mediums and psychics, is worth pondering.

Envoi

So where do I stand today about the real Allison DuBois and other research mediums?

As far as I can tell, they have an extraordinary and genuine gift. They can do specific things with their minds—getting accurate information about deceased loved ones—that I had been educated to believe was impossible. They are not frauds or cheats; quite the contrary, they are more genuine than many who write about them, or the professional skeptics who categorically dismiss them.

Yes, there are fraudulent mediums, just as there are fraudulent skeptics, lying media personalities, and even deceptive scientists. The key always is the challenge of discerning who is telling the truth.

- Is the available evidence provided by research mediums consistent with survival of consciousness after death? Absolutely.
- Is survival of consciousness the most promising explanation that accounts for the largest amount of the data? Clearly.
- Do the current experiments provide definitive proof of survival? No.
- Is it possible to design future experiments that can establish

once and for all if survival of consciousness is real? My strong conclusion, based on the evidence, is yes.

- Am I open to discovering in future experiments that the survival of consciousness hypothesis is mistaken? Of course.

The bottom line in science is a solemn—if not sacred—commitment to the evidence obtained through the conduct of valid, controlled, and replicated experiments. The cross we bear as genuine scientists is to follow the findings, wherever they lead, and to change our minds accordingly.

With this caveat in mind, it is appropriate for me to make a prediction—which, for the record, could be mistaken.

Based upon almost ten years of research on mediumship and the survival of consciousness after death, my prediction is that the kinds of findings revealed in this book will not go away, and that continuing evidence for "discarnate intention" will emerge because it is a real phenomenon.

Furthermore, my prediction is that the next wave of research mediums will be even more advanced in their skills and knowledge and will go beyond their teachers. Finally, my prediction is that those of us who hunger for understanding the existence of life and the meaning of love will at some point be able to celebrate the reality of spirit and soul, and the magnificent intelligence of a universe that has equipped our species with the potential to discover scientifically this fundamental spiritual truth.

The journey continues.

Life is a series of surprises, and would not be worth taking or keeping if it were not.

—Ralph Waldo Emerson

Acknowledgments

The truth is, I did not expect or plan to write this book. In March of 2005, my writing partner Bill Simon and I were working on the third book in our "Experiments" series—the first two were *The Afterlife Experiments* (2003) and *The G.O.D. Experiments* (forthcoming)—when a surprise occurred. After NBC's *Medium* television series took off, people from all walks of life—from scientists and the media to skeptics and my brother—were contacting me with the same two questions: Is Allison DuBois for real? And is the television show a real depiction of events in her life?

In the process of answering these two questions, again and again, it became clear to me that something in writing was needed. Most of the experiments—both informal and formal—involving Allison DuBois had not yet been published. Allison was frustrated, rightfully so, because much of the research involving her and other mediums was not in print. She understood that, as a university professor and director of a lab with a large NIH grant, I was a very busy person. She appreciated that mediumship was not my primary research area in terms of time responsibilities or funding, and that at least 50% of the mediumship experiments we ran, though theoretically and practically very important, were too exploratory to be published, by themselves, in conservative scientific journals. Nonetheless she wanted to have the research available for the public, including scientists, to read. What was I to do?

It occurred to me that maybe the time was right to write a book that reported a representative sample of research involving Allison. She wisely recommended that the book include findings from other mediums, not simply to document their credibility and help them with their evolving careers, but also to help establish both the validity and generality of the findings. She even said in an e-mail to me that were I to decide to write such a book, she would endorse it.

Bill Simon, who shares masthead credit with me on these books, is a masterful writer, a wonderful organizer, and a dear friend. I smile when I write books with him. And our agent, Bill Gladstone, is an agent's agent—how many in his business attended Yale and Harvard, are math whizzes, are wise and responsible when it comes to business, and are spiritual to boot?

My biggest thanks go to Allison, Bill S., Bill G., and Robert Friedman, the President of Hampton Roads Press, who together conspired to make this book a reality. The totality of their talent and energy has worked wonders.

I have been blessed to have worked with many gifted mediums, including highly visible ones like John Edward and less visible ones like Laurie Campbell. I need not repeat their names here since they are described in the book. These individuals know how much I appreciate all their efforts to help advance this work, as well as, in the process, to help educate this agnostic scientist about the reality of what they do. They also understand that I can never take what they say, or what anyone else says, at face value. The proof must be in the pudding, so to speak, and I need not only to see the pudding, but to taste it myself. As this book attests, these mediums have given me heaping plates of pudding to taste. Though some of the mediums have moved on—including Allison, Laurie, George, and Sally—others have moved in.

I have also been blessed to have worked with many remarkable research sitters. You have met some of them in this book. I want to acknowledge Hazel Courteney and Veronica Keen for their special contributions to the work. (See Hazel's 2005 book *The Evidence for the Sixth Sense.*) Also, I wish to especially thank Bob and Phran Ginsberg, who took their personal loss and research experience and created the visionary Forever Family Foundation (www.foreverfamily-foundation.org). They serve as a continued source of inspiration and guidance for this work.

My deepest thanks go to Dr. Julie Beischel, the William James Postdoctoral Fellow in Mediumship and Survival Research, for her assistance, collaboration, and support. The future of afterlife science is in its young investigators. Over the next few years Julie's significant contributions will become well known. Both Julie and I thank Dr. Peter Hayes, who not only personally funded Julie's fellowship, but has served as a "voice of sanity" providing important creative as well as critical advice and counsel to the research.

Some of this research was inspired and funded by the John Kaspari Fund. Bill has been an ardent supporter and has participated as a research sitter as well as an advisor. A retired engineer and president of a biomedical company, Bill is concerned with both science and facts. Some of this research was also funded by Michael and Norma Knopf, in honor of their late son, and their support is gratefully acknowledged.

The University of Arizona has played an important role in enabling this work to go forward. At the time this book was written, key administrators—from President Peter Likins of the University of Arizona and President Richard Imwalle of the University of Arizona Foundation, through Dr. Richard Powell, former senior Vice President for Research, Dr. Edward Donnerstein, Dean of the College of Social and Behavioral Sciences, and Dr. Allan Kaszniak, Head of the Psychology Department—have each come to the defense of academic freedom and the commitment to pursuing important questions in a creative, comprehensive, and careful manner. They have steadfastly protected the right of faculty to conduct (and the responsibility of universities to allow) controversial research into what are among the most important questions facing humanity: Do humans have souls? Does our consciousness survive physical death? And can certain individuals (mediums) accurately receive information from those who have passed over? As you read in Chapter 9, Drs. Likins and Imwalle have faced the wrath of professional skeptics with dignity and grace.

Many of my colleagues who are associated with the Center for Frontier Medicine in Biofield Science at the University of Arizona—in departments ranging from psychology and optical sciences to psychiatry and surgery—have provided valuable encouragement and invaluable criticism during the period of this research. Some are enthusiastic about the work and are glad it is flourishing; others are less enthusiastic (partly because it is so controversial). Also, I have been blessed to work with a number of excellent graduate students as well as staff. I extend my heartfelt thanks to Dr. Iris Bell, Dr. Audrey Brooks, Sheryl Attig, Katie Reece, Gerry Nangel, Dr. Melinda Connor, Dr. Cheryl Ritenbaugh, Dr. Mikel Aickin, Dr. Ernie Schloss, Tomoe Lombard, Clarissa Siebern, Willow Sibert, Dr. Allan Hamilton, Dr. Lonnie Nelson, Dan Lewis, Sabrina Lewis, Dr. Kathy Creath, Dr. Katharine Burleson, and Dr. Richard Lane. I don't know what I would do without you.

A subset of the women—scientists, students, and staff—who are thankfully tough and gratefully caring about protecting me and the work recently decided to create "Gary's Angels"—proving that they not only are dedicated but have a silly sense of humor.

Numerous scientists who perform research in controversial science and know what it is like firsthand to be on the firing line have contributed, directly or indirectly, to our mediumship research. Notable are Dr. Rupert Sheldrake, Dr. Dean Radin, Dr. Emily Kelly, Dr. Edward Kelly, Dr. Bruce Greyson, Dianne Arcangel, Dr. Konstantine Korotkov, Dr. Steven Grenard, and Dr. Donald Watson. Your ideas resound in my mind.

I also thank a number of professional skeptics who remind me to be careful and "watch my back" every step of the way; they include Dr. Ray Hymen, Dr. Michael Shermer, Dr. Paul Kurtz, and James Randi.

Among the most remarkable and memorable of the surprises

that have occurred in the process of doing this work has been the unexpected meeting of some gifted persons who have played behind-the-scenes roles, offering me their exceptional intelligence, substantial experience, and enlightened wisdom. They include Dr. Linda Van Dyke, Dr. Suzanne Mendelssohn, Dr. Edgar Mitchell, Dr. Jeanette Renouf, and Dr. Diane Powell. Each of you, in your own way, has made an invaluable difference in my life and this work.

Finally, the most extraordinary and unforgettable of the surprises appear to come from "the other side." The truth is, this research would be meaningless (if not a complete failure) were it not for the dedicated individuals who have "passed on" but apparently not "passed away." They include Susy Smith, Dr. William James, Bailey Ginsberg, Princess Diana, Montague Keen, Dr. John Mack, as well as Howard and Shirley Schwartz.

Our future books on mediums and afterlife science will reveal the extraordinary unexpected evidence these people and others appear to continue to provide for "discarnate intention." The conventional scientist might complain that these particular observations are "uncontrolled," meaning uncontrolled by the experimenter(s). However, I believe that in time we will be able to show that this is the case because it is the "deceased"—and not us, the experimenters—who are actually "in control" of the evidence.

Thanks to them, and to the universe that makes all this possible, the journey continues and the surprises unfold.

Appendix A

A Long-Distance Internet Mediumship Experiment Involving the "Double-Deceased" Paradigm

By Gary E. Schwartz, Human Energy Systems Laboratory, University of Arizona and Steven Grenard, Institute of Sleep Medicine, Staten Island University Hospital

This manuscript was originally written December 2002 with the title "Accuracy and Specificity for Long-Distance Internet Mediumship: The 'Double-Deceased' Multi-Medium Paradigm." Updated in May 2005.

Abstract

Recent research suggests that certain mediums can obtain accurate and specific information about deceased persons long-distance via the Internet (Grenard and Schwartz, 2002). The present report replicates and extends long-distance Internet mediumship research using a novel "double-deceased" paradigm. In the experiment, three evidence-based mediums (located in Arizona, Missouri, and New York) were asked to attempt to contact one deceased person, SS, with whom they had previously been successful in obtaining specific and accurate information. The procedure involved the first author, in his thoughts, requesting that the deceased SS bring a second deceased person, KGN, to the three mediums for a reading. The three mediums conducted these readings in the privacy of their homes and e-mailed the information to GS, who forwarded the information to SG (the sitter, in New York) for scoring. The mediums were not told the identity of the second deceased person or the identity of the sitter. The items were scored using a -3 to +3 scale by the sitter (SG) as well as the control (GS). The average +3 percent accuracy ratings of the three readings for the sitter (SG) was 67%, compared with 23% for the control (GS) ($p < .004$). Careful analysis of the content reveals that the totality of the findings cannot be explained as rater bias. The double-deceased paradigm generates findings that question the plausibility of purported super-psi explanations. Long-distance multi-center, double-blind experiments can be conducted using the double-deceased paradigm.

Introduction

In recent years, a small group of scientists have examined the possible validity of carefully selected mediums obtaining accurate and specific information via anomalous/paranormal mechanisms. Schwartz and colleagues at the University of Arizona have conducted a series of single-blind experiments with well-known mediums, including John Edward, the host and medium of the daily television program *Crossing Over* (Edward, 2001), George Anderson, the medium featured in *Contact* (Anderson, 2000), and Allison DuBois (DuBois, 2005), whose life inspired the NBC television show *Medium*. Edward and Anderson, along with Suzane Northrop (Northrop, 2002), Anne Gehman, and Laurie Campbell, were studied by Schwartz and colleagues (Schwartz et al., 2001); the procedures and basic findings were shown on the documentary *Life Afterlife* (HBO, 1999).

These preliminary experiments were reviewed in Schwartz (2002). Recent experiments included multi-sitter/multi-medium paradigms; the latest experiments were conducted double-blind and long-distance (e.g., Schwartz et al., 2003). Even under conditions where the sitters could not be seen by the mediums and also did not speak (i.e., the sitters provided no visual or auditory cues), accurate and specific information was obtained by this select group of mediums. Findings reported in Scotland (Robertson and Roy, 2001; Roy and Robertson, 2001) independently replicated and extended these findings and falsified the generalization hypothesis with odds against chance of 5.37×10^{-11}.

It is possible, in principle, to conduct long-distance mediumship experiments using the Internet. A demonstration Internet-chat room mediumship experiment was conducted by Grenard and Schwartz (2002). Ten mediums in various locations across the United States, in over more than twenty sessions, provided long-distance Internet chat-room readings with one sitter (SG) primarily concerning one deceased person (KGN). In addition, face-to-face (or telephone) readings with three "trance" mediums (one located in England) provided confirmatory evidence.

GS reviewed SG's scoring to determine if rater bias was a plausible explanation for the totality of the findings. The level of specificity and detail for a substantial subset of the items ruled out concluding that the findings could be explained entirely in terms of general statements that would be rated positively by raters.

The present paper reports the results of an experiment using a novel "double-deceased" paradigm that can readily be conducted long-distance. The Internet is employed here as a means of rapidly providing information to the experimenters and, subsequently, to the sitters. The structure of the paradigm questions the plausibility of using speculated super-psi mechanisms as an explanation of the findings.

The double-deceased paradigm was discovered by GS in the context of an unanticipated long-distance e-mail reading by Janet Mayer. The general paradigm can be outlined as follows:

1. Research sitters are chosen who are willing to perform item-by-item scoring of readings obtained via the Internet. The research sitters are kept blind to the identity of the research sitters as well as the times that the readings are conducted (see below).

2. The experimenter is kept blind to details about the deceased loved ones of the sitters as well as the times that the readings are conducted (see below).
3. The experimenter attempts to contact, in his mind, one deceased person (a "departed hypothesized co-investigator"—DHCI) and requests the DHCI to bring the sitter's deceased loved ones to research mediums who have previously read the DHCI successfully (i.e., it has been previously documented that the research mediums can obtain accurate information about the DHCI).
4. The research mediums, at times selected by the mediums (and known only by them), in the privacy of their homes, attempt to (a) contact the DHCI, and then (b) conduct a reading of the deceased individual(s) purportedly introduced to them by the DHCI. The mediums are kept blind to the identity of the sitters and their locations.
5. The research mediums e-mail their readings to the experimenter, who forwards the item-by-item information of the readings to the sitters.

The double-decease paradigm makes a number of core assumptions that are open to question:

1. That DHCIs exist.
2. That DHCIs agree to perform their role as co-investigators in the experiment.
3. That DHCIs can detect the thoughts of the experimenters.
4. That DHCIs can "locate and bring" the sitters' deceased loved ones to the designated research mediums
5. That the research mediums can contact the DHCIs and then read the deceased persons purportedly introduced by the DHCIs.

The present paper presents the findings from an experiment that illustrates the potential utility and significance of the double-deceased paradigm for testing the survival of consciousness hypothesis.

Method

Subjects

The research "sitter" was SG. He is Director of Research for the Institute of Sleep Medicine at the Staten Island University Hospital. The age- and sex-matched control rater was GS, who is Director of the Human Energy Systems Laboratory at the University of Arizona.

Departed Hypothesized Co-Investigator (DHCI)

The DHCI was the late Susy Smith, author of thirty books in parapsychology and survival of consciousness after death (reviewed in Smith, 2000). Evidence consistent with Smith serving as a DHCI has been reported in previous experiments (Schwartz et al., 1999; Schwartz and Russek, 2001; Schwartz, Russek, and Geoffrion, 2001; Schwartz and Chopra, 2002; Schwartz et al., 2002).

Primary Deceased Persons

The primary deceased person purportedly brought to the mediums by the DHCI for the sitter (SG) was his son KNG, who died in 2001 at age 33. The DHCI was not requested to bring a deceased person for the control rater (GS).

Experimenter

The experimenter was GS. He was in New York at the time he made the requests to the DHCI. He was in Arizona during the scoring of the experiment.

Mediums

Three evidence-based mediums (EBMs) participated.

1. Janet Mayer (JM), from Saint Louis, Missouri. She co-discovered the double-deceased paradigm with GS in the process of conducting over 300 long-distance readings with the DHCI from April 2001 to October 2002.
2. Mary Occhino (MO), from Long Island, New York. She participated in two other long-distance experiments, one with the DHCI (Schwartz et al, 2002; Schwartz and Chopra, 2002).

3. Allison DuBois (AD), from Phoenix, Arizona. She participated in multiple pilot studies with the DHCI (e.g., Schwartz, Russek, and Geoffrion, 2001), including one long-distance study with the DHCI (Schwartz and Chopra, 2002).

Experimental Designs

The design was a multi-medium, single-sitter experiment. GS requested that the DHCI bring the deceased KNG to the three EBMs while GS was in New York. Their readings were e-mailed to GS. The e-mails were forwarded to SG by GS for scoring when GS returned to Arizona.

Scoring

Each initial, name, historical fact, appearance description, temperament description, personal opinion, and so forth was scored using the following 7-point scale: -3, definite miss; -2, probable miss; -1, possible miss; 0, maybe no, maybe yes; +1, possible hit; +2, probable hit; +3, definite hit.

SG and GS each scored the three readings independently.

Results

Figure 1 displays the percent scores for the seven ratings, averaged across the three EBMs, separately for SG (the sitter) and GS (the control).

It can be seen that the average +3 percent score for SG (the solid sitter line) was 67%, compared with 23% for GS (the dashed control line). Conversely, the average -3 percent score for SG was 3%, compared with 35% for GS.

A 2 x 7 analysis of variance with sitter versus control (2) as a between-subject factor and percent scores (7) as a within-subject factor (repeated measure) yielded a highly significant sitter versus control by percent scores interaction ($F(6, 24)=12.859$, $p<.000001$).

The reason for the high p value is that each of the three EBMs yielded similar results. Figure 2 displays bar graphs for the individual EBMs for the +3 percent accuracy ratings.

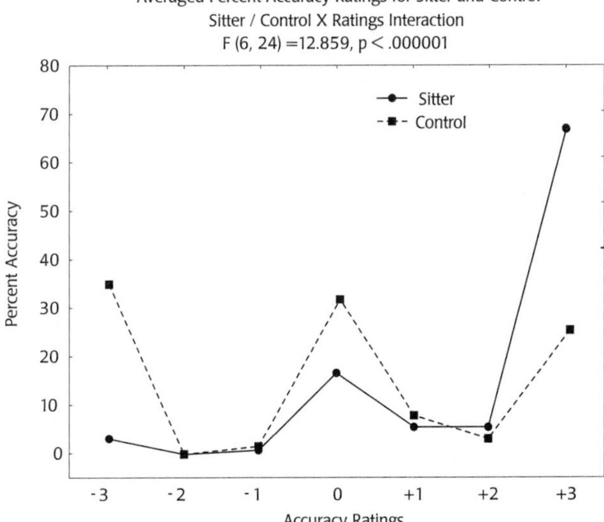

Figure 1

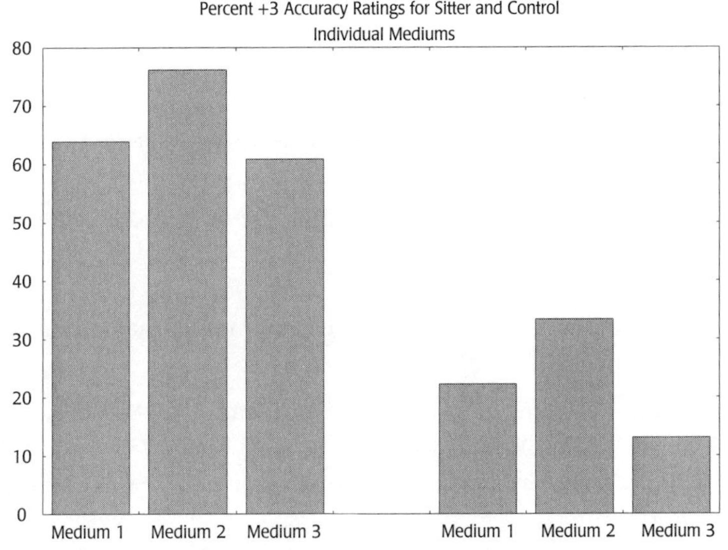

Figure 2

A one-way analysis of variance is significant ($F(1, 4)=34.537$, $p<.004$).

Additional analyses were performed to examine the possibility that the results were due to ratings of general items versus specific items.

GS coded the items 0 if general and 1 if specific. Using these codes, the items were sorted and averages were calculated.

Examples of general items included:

- Male child (vague)
- Nurse (no reference)
- Railroad connection (vague)
- Older male living (very general)
- Mild tempered (widely applicable)
- Some balding (vague)
- Michael (a common name)

Examples of specific items included:

- Grandfather had a harmonica (specific object attached to specific person)
- MIT (specific university)
- Intestinal cancer cause of death in male connected to deceased (specific cause attached to specific person)
- Buddha statue (specific object)
- Special ring-membership/fraternity tie-in (specific object and significance)
- Make sure fish in aquarium are cared for
- Sarah "for the above" (relatively uncommon name attached to specific person)

For the three mediums combined, 46 items were coded as general and 57 were coded as specific.

Figure 3 displays the findings for the sitter (left box) and the control (right box).

The pattern of findings displayed in Figure 3 suggests that sitter ratings of general information versus specific information cannot explain the differences observed between the sitter and the control.

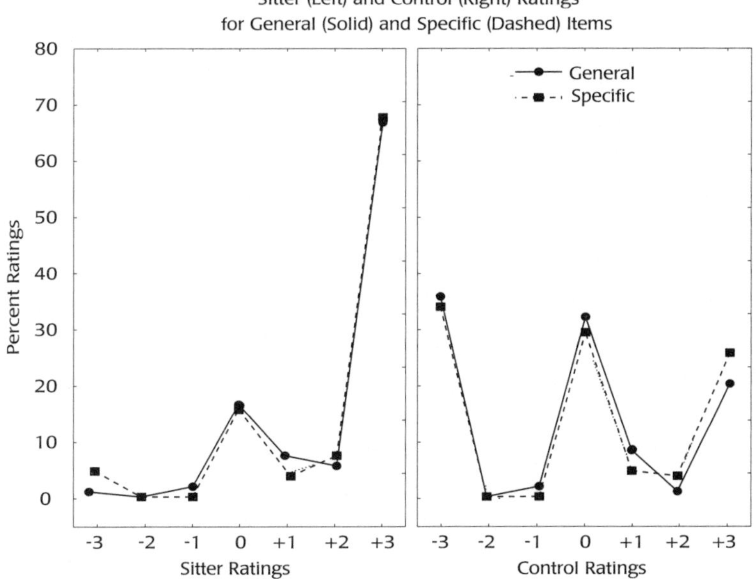

Figure 3

Discussion

The present findings replicate and extend previous research indicating that long-distance readings, conducted under single-blind conditions (i.e., where the medium does not know either the identity or the location of the sitter) can yield accurate and specific information (e.g., Schwartz and Russek, 2001; Grenard and Schwartz, 2002).

The present findings cannot be explained in terms of fraud (i.e., pre-reading information), cold reading, visual or auditory cues, or sensory leakage.

In addition, the totality of the findings cannot be explained as sitter rater bias, given the inclusion of highly specific information in the readings information that applied uniquely to the sitter versus his age- and sex-matched control.

The double-deceased paradigm poses substantial difficulties for purported super-psi hypotheses.

First, it is not plausible to explain the present findings as mind reading of the experimenter, per se, since GS had virtually no knowledge of the history of SG's deceased loved one. The experimental design rules out this speculation.

Second, in order to explain the present findings as due to mind reading of the sitter, the mediums in this experiment would have had to (1) first read the mind of the experimenter (getting both the first and last names of the sitter accurately, as well as his address), (2) then locate the sitter in the greater New York area, and (3) finally read the sitter's mind. There is no evidence that the mediums received the name of sitter—first or last (and mediums rarely get last names). (Also note: Since the mediums were blind to who the sitter was, they could not use this information to cheat and find information about the sitter on the Internet.)

In the double-deceased paradigm, not only does the experimenter serve as a "proxy" for the sitter; the "departed hypothesized co-investigator" can be thought of as a "deceased proxy" as well.

It is possible to add the double-deceased paradigm to multi-center, double-blind experiments. An initial dual-center, double-blind, double-deceased experiment with SS as one DHCI (the Arizona center) and KNG as a second DHCI (the New York center) has been completed and positive findings were obtained (Schwartz et al., in preparation).

Schwartz concluded in *The Afterlife Experiments* (Schwartz, 2002) that when the totality of the findings is considered, the most parsimonious explanation that accounts for the largest amount of the data—including the "dazzle shots"—is the survival of consciousness hypothesis. Following Ockham's razor, we suggest that the same conclusion can be applied to the totality of the data presented in this report.

Bibliography

Anderson, George and Andrew Barone. 2000. *Lessons from the Light: Extraordinary Messages of Comfort and Hope from the Other Side*. Berkley Publishing Group/Penguin Putnam, New York.

Berger, Arthur S. 1987. *Aristocracy of the Dead: New Findings in Postmortem Survival*. McFarland & Company, Jefferson, NC.

DuBois, Allison. 2005. *Don't Kiss Them Good-bye*. Fireside Book/Simon & Schuster, New York.

Edward, John. 2001. *Crossing Over: The Stories behind the Stories*. San Diego, Jodere Group.

Grenard, Steven, and Schwartz, Gary E. 2002. "Evidence of Accuracy and Specificity for Internet Mediumship: A Multi-Medium Multi-Experiment Series." Unpublished manuscript.

Keen, Montague. 2001. Letters. *Paranormal Review*, Number 20 (October), p.15.

Northrop, Suzane. 2002. *Second Chance: Healing Messages from the Afterlife*. San Diego, Jodere Group.

Robertson, Tricia J., and Roy, Archie E. 2001. "A Preliminary Study of the Acceptance by Non-Recipients of Mediums' Statements to Recipients." *Journal of the Society for Psychical Research*, 65.2, pp. 91-106.

Roy, Archie E., and Robertson, Tricia J. 2001. "A Double-Blind Procedure for Assessing the Relevance of a Medium's Statements to a Recipient." *Journal of the Society for Psychical Research*, 65.3, pp 161–174.

Schwartz, Gary E.R. Russek, Linda G.S., Nelson, Lonnie A., and Barentsen, Christopher. 2001. "Accuracy and Replicability of Anomalous After-Death Communication Across Highly Skilled Mediums." *Journal of the Society for Psychical Research*, 65.1, pp 1-25.

Schwartz, Gary E.R., and Russek, Linda G.S. 2001. "Evidence of Anomalous Information Retrieval Between Two Mediums: Telepathy, Network Memory Resonance, and Continuance of Consciousness." *Journal of the Society for Psychical Research*, 65.4, pp 257-276.

Schwartz, Gary E.R., Russek, Linda G.S., and Geoffrion, Sabrina. 2001. "Celebrating Susy Smith's Soul: Further Evidence for the

Continuance of Smith's Consciousness After Her Physical Death." *Journal of Religion and Psychical Research*, 24 (July), pp. 123-130.

Schwartz, Gary E., and Chopra, Deepak. 2002. "Nonlocal Anomalous Information Retrieval: A Multi-Medium Multi-Scored Single-Blind Experiment." Unpublished manuscript.

Schwartz, Gary, with Simon, William L. 2002. *The Afterlife Experiments: Breakthrough Scientific Evidence of Life After Death*. Simon & Schuster (Pocketbooks), New York.

Smith, Susy. 2000. *The Afterlife Codes*. Hampton Roads Publishing, Charlottesville, VA.

Appendix B

Survival Is in the Details: A Double-Blind and Single-Blind Experiment

Presented during "The Study of Mediumship: Interdisciplinary Perspectives" forum at the Omni Hotel, Charlottesville, Virginia, January 29-30, 2005. "Survival Is in the Details: Emerging Evidence for Discarnate Intention from Mediumship Research" by Gary E. Schwartz, Ph.D., and Julie Beischel, Ph.D., Human Energy Systems Laboratory, VERITAS Research Program, the University of Arizona.

Supported in part by the Peter Hayes Fund and the John Kaspari Fund. We thank Dr. Hayes and Mr. William Kaspari for their support as well as comments on the manuscript. The transcripts and commentary described in this paper were read verbatim as part of Dr. Schwartz's keynote address on June 27, 2004 at a tribute in London honoring Montague Keen; the graph and scoring included in this paper were also summarized at this public meeting. This paper is dedicated to Susy Smith and Montague Keen.

Abstract

Contemporary experiments at the University of Arizona using single-blind and double-blind protocols with research mediums have provided compelling evidence for anomalous information retrieval (Schwartz Gary E., *The Afterlife Experiments,* 2002). Gifted mediums can obtain highly specific information under experimental conditions that rule out conventional explanations such as fraud, cold reading, sitter/rater bias, and experimenter error.

Current research includes (1) long-distance experiments where the mediums, experimenters, and sitters are separated by hundreds or thousands of miles, (2) proxy-sitter experiments where the experimenter serves as the proxy sitter and the absent sitter does not know when the actual reading is taking place, (3) e-mail experiments where the experimenter does not know when the actual reading is taking place, and (4) "double-deceased" designs where one deceased person (termed a "departed hypothesized co-investigator") is requested to bring a second deceased person to a given medium. However, these experiments, by themselves, do not distinguish among alternative paranormal explanations such as telepathy, super-psi, and/or survival of consciousness after death.

Careful analysis of the transcripts from these experiments reveals unanticipated and uncontrolled—yet replicated—anomalous events implying *discarnate intention* that virtually rule out both telepathy and super-psi as plausible explanations of the totality of the findings. Four major classes of these *apparent discarnate intention events* that have emerged in our research are:

1. *Drop-Ins*—Evidential information regarding unanticipated, uninvited, and sometimes unknown individuals who appear in specific readings;
2. *Interruptions*—Evidential information that interrupts experimenter-initiated questions (implying intentional direction and effort from the purported deceased communicant);
3. *Cross-Correspondence*—Evidential information that fits across readings as well as within readings; and

4. *Selective Withholding of Information*—Evidential information that appears to be intentionally withheld across and within readings.

Evidence regarding spontaneous interruptions in research involving Allison DuBois as the research medium is described in detail here, as well as analyses of the double-blind portion of the experiment. Careful analyses of the wording and semantics from transcripts concerning the late Montague Keen provide additional evidence consistent with the survival of consciousness hypothesis.

The full article describing this study can be found at the author's Web site at ***http://veritas.arizona.edu/survivaldetails.htm.***

> *If you wish to upset the law that all crows are black, you must not seek to show that no crows are; it is enough if you prove one single crow to be white.*
>
> *—William James, M.D.*

> *He's kind of laughing and he's like "way to go out," like "way to leave this world, right there and then," because who better than the person that died to know that he would be where he is, that he would be in a good place, who better than him?*
>
> *—Allison DuBois, Research Medium*

> *The general view among scientists that novel phenomena must be fitted into an explanatory framework or hypothesis for them to be taken other than as an epiphenomenon or oddity is illogical and should be ignored.*
>
> *—Montague Keen*

Appendix C
Representative Readings and Websites on Mediumship

Below are a few examples of books and Websites that together provide a useful introduction to the science and art of mediumship.

Books by Scientists and Philosophers

Braude, Stephen E. (2003). *Immortal Remains: The Evidence of Life after Death.*

Gauld, Alan (1984). *Mediumship and Survival: A Century of Investigations.*

Schwartz, Gary E. with Simon, William L. (2002). *The Afterlife Experiments: Breakthrough Scientific Evidence for Life after Death.*

Books by Mediums

Dalzell, George (2002). *Messages: Evidence for Life after Death.*

DuBois, Allison (2005). *Don't Kiss Them Good-Bye.*

Occhino, Mary (2004). *Within These Four Walls.*

Educational Websites

foreverfamilyfoundation.org (public service site with newsletters and links)

survivalafterdeath.org (comprehensive site with historical readings and links)

veritas.arizona.edu (university site with original research, readings and links)

Index

Y

Z

About the Authors

Gary E. Schwartz has a Ph.D. in personality psychology from Harvard and was a professor of psychology and psychiatry at Yale before joining the University of Arizona, where he teaches and directs the Human Energy Systems Laboratory. He is the author of *The Afterlife Experiments* and *The Living Energy Universe*. He lives in Tucson.

William L. Simon has written and coauthored more than a dozen books, including Schwartz's previous book, *The Afterlife Experiments*, as well as *iCon: Steve Jobs* and *The Art of Intrusion*. He lives in Los Angeles.

Hampton Roads Publishing Company

... for the evolving human spirit

HAMPTON ROADS PUBLISHING COMPANY publishes books on a variety of subjects, including metaphysics, spirituality, health, visionary fiction, and other related topics.

For a copy of our latest trade catalog, call toll-free, 800-766-8009, or send a request with your name and address to:

HAMPTON ROADS PUBLISHING COMPANY, INC.
1125 STONEY RIDGE ROAD • CHARLOTTESVILLE, VA 22902
e-mail: hrpc@hrpub.com • Internet: www.hrpub.com